DOGS OF THE
HINTERLAND

TINA SHAW

Published by Pearson Education Limited, Edinburgh Gate, Harlow, Essex, CM20 2JE
Registered company number: 872828

www.pearsonschools.co.uk

First published by Pearson Education New Zealand
a division of Pearson New Zealand Ltd
67 Apollo Drive, Rosedale, North Shore 0632, New Zealand
Associated companies throughout the world

Text © Pearson Education New Zealand 2008

Page layout and Design: Suzanne Wesley

The right of Tina Shaw to be identified as author of this work has been asserted by
her in accordance with the Copyright, Designs and Patents Act 1988.

First published 2008
This edition published 2012

15 14 13 12
10 9 8 7 6 5 4 3 2

British Library Cataloguing in Publication Data
A catalogue record for this book is available from the British Library

ISBN: 978-0-43507-616-0

Printed and bound in Malaysia (CTP-VP)

Acknowledgements
We would like to thank the children and teachers of Bangor Central Integrated
Primary School, NI; Bishop Henderson C of E Primary School, Somerset; Brookside
Community Primary School, Somerset; Cheddington Combined School,
Buckinghamshire; Cofton Primary School, Birmingham; Dair House Independent
School, Buckinghamshire; Deal Parochial School, Kent; Lawthorn Primary School,
North Ayrshire; Newbold Riverside Primary School, Rugby and Windmill Primary
School, Oxford for their invaluable help in the development and trialling of the Bug
Club resources.

Every effort has been made to contact copyright holders of material reproduced in
this book. Any omissions will be rectified in subsequent printings if notice is given
to the publishers.

A division of Pearson New Zealand Ltd

PROLOGUE

The old man laughed softly and held up a single finger. Vancy stared at him in fascination and horror. "Let me tell you a story," he began, his voice deep and low. "A baby was once born here and a prophecy was made about this baby. The prophecy told that one day, in the future, when the baby had grown into a young woman, she would destroy this fortress. So the baby was ... disposed of – left out in the desert to die. At least, that was what they thought at the time. But later, much later, it seemed that she had lived."

The large, silver dog sat on his haunches in the twilight, remembering a baby left in the desert to die. And he remembered saving that babe by carrying her across the Hinterland to the village of Bassorah. For this was no ordinary dog. He had memory and he could "speak" with humans – make himself understood. All of his pack could.

There had always been silver dogs in the Hinterland and the plains beyond the mountains. Many years ago, perhaps a hundred years before, a pair of dogs had come to this land. They found a cave in a sheltered position and made it their home. Over time, the pack grew and grew.

The dogs watched as men came and went. Mostly the men left the dogs alone. They saw the dark Fortress being built on top of stone.

But now, fifteen years after saving that baby, the leader of the silver dogs was anxious. Things were happening that he didn't like. An unnatural force was moving in the world, and he felt powerless to stop it . . .

I

The Patrol was walking back to the cliff-ringed village of Bassorah when one of the party stopped and looked back. The man squinted, surveying the Hinterland. The barren plains were dim with the coming night. Yet, in the far distance, he could make out a dark shape coming their way. There was the sound of hooves.

The others, too, had stopped. "Spread out," hissed Merta, their leader.

The group quickly separated and hunched down, blending into the twilight gloom. From a distance, clad as they were in browns and greys, they looked like boulders among the tussock.

A man on a horse, moving slowly, was coming out of the gloom. As his horse neared one of the Patrol, it suddenly reared, stamping its feet. A rope sang out, flying swiftly through the air, lassoing the rider around the middle.

"Hey!" he cried out. "What the . . . "

A fierce-looking woman stood up from the ground and levelled a spear at the rider. "Speak out your name!"

"I . . . I am the emissary of Herit," said the frightened man in a high-pitched voice. "I have an important message for Bassorah. Please, spare my life!"

The Patrol gathered closer and the woman held a brief muttered debate with two of the men.

"What is the nature of this message?" the woman demanded.

The man squirmed in his saddle. "That is for your Council to hear."

Another muttered conference. The man holding the rope pulled it tighter, just in case.

"Dismount," said the woman, "and we will take you to them."

Vancy was hurrying to feed the mill ponies. This was usually her favourite part of the day – putting fresh straw in the stables, checking their water, talking to each of the ponies in turn. But this evening it was different. Even the ponies could sense her excitement. They were skittish around the girl, nuzzling her urgently with their soft noses.

"All right, all right," she said, "there's enough for everyone." Using the fork, Vancy lifted a bundle of straw onto the shelf in the stables. One of the ponies gave her a little nip. "Hey, what was that for?" she cried. She had never been nipped before. But then, she had never had a coming-of-age party before, either. She was as nervous as a goose.

With the straw in place, she hurried out of the pony enclosure, shutting the gate carefully behind her. Then she ran – down the cobbled street that formed the centre of the town of Bassorah and past the small stone houses, where lights were beginning to show. It wouldn't do to be late for her own party! Especially as the Council had granted special permission for her to have one.

For as long as anybody could remember, only the true Bassorah people had a coming-of-age party when they turned fifteen. Having arrived here as a baby, Vancy had always been considered an outsider in the community. Not of the blood.

Huh! But she'd shown them that you could be one of them, even if you weren't of the blood. Bloodlines weren't everything. There was also such a thing as loyalty. Besides, her foster parents, Erik and Lisbet, were true Bassorah people. That should have counted for something, and maybe, finally, it had.

The girl raced into one of the houses, narrowly avoiding an enormous plate of jellies on a small table by the door.

"Vancy, it's nearly time." It was Lisbet, wringing her hands. "Where have you been?"

"Nowhere," she gasped, running for her room.

She grabbed the jug of water on her table and splashed some of it into a large bowl. A quick rinse later, Vancy pulled off her grimy old shirt and changed it for a clean one. Lisbet had wanted to make her a dress for the party, but Vancy refused to wear dresses.

Back in the living area, she came to a halt, feeling as highly strung as one of her ponies. The room had been readied for all the people who would soon be arriving at their house. In the kitchen area, the table was covered with platters of fruit and sweetmeats.

Erik stepped in from the courtyard and, seeing Vancy, grinned. "Well, here you are," he said quietly. He went over and put his hands on her shoulders. "Are you ready for your big night?"

"Don't know," she muttered.

Erik nodded. "I'm very proud of you, my daughter."

The girl ducked her chin as a warm flush of pleasure and embarrassment rushed over her face. A knock on the door saved her from having to reply and Lisbet hurried to open it. "They're here," she muttered, "they're here."

The door would be left open so that all the guests could enter the house freely throughout the evening. It seemed as if the entire community of Bassorah was squeezing into their little house, though Vancy knew that couldn't be right. Some people still had to keep watch at the Keep and go out on the evening's Patrol. Some cake would be saved for those who couldn't come.

People were congratulating Vancy and bringing in more food.

Suddenly, a loud voice called out and a hand could be seen waving over the heads. "Oi, Vancy," shouted Kerei, unceremoniously pushing his way through. He clapped her on the back. "Isn't this great? Your own coming-of-age party."

"Oh, it's no big deal," she lied.

"No big deal!" Kerei exclaimed. "You've got to be kidding. It's the best party of your life. And now you're an adult."

"What, like you?" she teased. Kerei had had his own coming-of-age party only a few months before, and Vancy hadn't seen much difference in him since.

Nevertheless, he puffed out his chest. "Yes," he said. "Look at me. I'm on the Watch now. It sure beats looking after those evil ponies of yours."

"Walking up and down all night with a lantern," scoffed Vancy. "It's not my idea of a good job."

"You'd be surprised how interesting walking around with a lantern can be," the boy retorted. "In fact . . . " Kerei's train of thought was interrupted by a plate of almond patties going past. He shot out a hand and managed to grab two of them before the plate moved on.

More people were squeezing into the living area. Others were flowing out into the rear courtyard and the guitarist had perched himself in a corner and started a lively tune. A ginger-haired boy appeared next to Vancy, holding out a bunch of flowers.

"Congratulations," he said.

"Thank you, Squirt," the girl murmured. Vancy had never been given flowers before. She buried her nose in the bunch to hide her blush.

"I'm glad that you came back to Bassorah with us that time," he said quite formally, as if it was a speech he had prepared.

Kerei nudged him. "Of course she came back – we rescued her, didn't we?"

Vancy snorted and nearly whacked him over the head with the flowers. "I was doing perfectly all right by myself, lizard brain."

"Listen to that," the boy exclaimed in mock horror. "You're supposed to be nice to people at your coming-of-age party."

"I was being nice," said Vancy.

Erik was making his way through the crowd towards her. "Come, we are going to perform the ritual now." He took Vancy's hand and led her outside.

It was a Bassorah tradition for the father and his friends to carry the child who was coming of age across the threshold of the house. It was meant to mark the end of childhood. When Vancy next walked across the threshold, they said, she would be a woman.

Then there would be their funny dancing, where everybody linked arms and kicked their way around the room. Lisbet, who had been worrying about the furniture for days, had moved nearly all of it into the other rooms.

Vancy waited quietly with her foster father and thought about the journey she and the boys had made only a few months ago across the Hinterland to the Fortress. She had run away, seeking her real parents. She may not have found her mother, but she had found out what became of her. And she had found an uncle. Tem was outside in the courtyard now, organising the special music that would accompany Erik and Vancy into the house. She could already hear his flute beginning the first notes of the melody. And now here she was, turning fifteen and having her own party. She shook her head. It all seemed too unreal. A feeling of gratitude flowed through her as she looked around at the happy, smiling faces – these were her people. She glanced up at Erik's glowing face.

"Are you ready?" he asked quietly.

Vancy nodded. Her foster father and his friends hoisted her up onto their shoulders.

Herit's messenger stood in the middle of the room, hands clasped nervously in front of him. He was dressed in the typical Fortress garb of black leather, with silver armbands that glittered in the flickering light from the lanterns. An empty knife scabbard, also decorated in silver, hung at his side. A sound of music came from the distance – Vancy's party was still in full swing – but in the Council room there was only a heavy silence.

The Council – three men and two women – sat

on chairs facing the stranger, their eyes unreadable in the dim light. The man shuffled nervously.

"You have a message from Herit," one of them finally said. "Speak it now."

The messenger cleared his throat. "These are the words of Herit," he said, striking a fist to his chest. "I wish for my blood daughter, Vancy, to be returned to me."

The two women exchanged sharp glances.

"She shall be Princess Regent and, on my death, shall inherit my lands," said the man in a loud voice, his chin proudly raised. "In exchange, I shall leave the fine people of Bassorah in peace. If, however, you do not look favourably upon my request, then I shall take my daughter by force. The choice is yours, Bassorah. This I proclaim!" The man lowered his eyes to the floor, waiting for their response.

One of the Council spoke into the stunned pause. "Is that all?"

"There is no more," said the man. "Do you require me to repeat the message?"

"It is a simple message," said one of the women drily. "I think we have understood Herit's meaning."

One of the Council rose from his seat and nodded to the armed woman standing near the door. "Merta, take this messenger to the Keep and see that he is given refreshments." He then addressed Herit's man. "We will give you our answer in the morning."

When the messenger and his escort had left the room, the Council stood and gathered together to confer.

"Do you think Herit will keep his promise and leave us alone?" The speaker's voice was filled with hope. For too many years, Bassorah – a fertile, protected valley ringed by cliffs – had been threatened by Herit. Was it possible that he would finally give up trying to steal their land, their water supply and fertile soil from them?

"It would be a miracle," said another of the men.

The two women, who had been speaking quickly and softly together, now broke apart. One of them stepped forward, frowning. "A miracle, maybe," she protested, "but the price would be paid by Vancy."

"Impossible," said the Leader.

"We mustn't even tell her . . . " said another.

"No, she must be warned – we must all be on our guard."

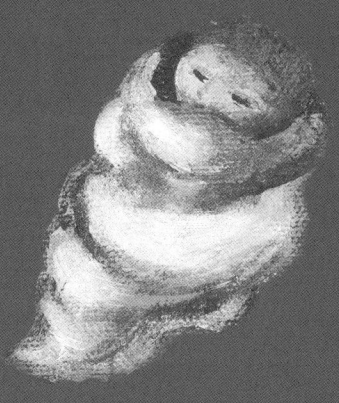

II

It was late and everybody had left. Vancy, still keyed up from the party, was helping Lisbet to tidy the house before they went to bed. Erik had already disappeared. A sharp rap on the door made them both look up.

"Somebody's probably forgotten something," said Lisbet, going to open the door.

A shadowy figure loomed on the doorstep and spoke to Lisbet for several minutes in a low voice. Vancy wandered across the room, straining to recognise the voice.

"But is that really necessary tonight?" Vancy heard Lisbet ask.

"What is necessary tonight?" asked Vancy, joining her foster mother at the door. The Leader of the Council was standing solemnly on the threshold, dimly lit by the light from the house. For no reason,

Vancy felt a cool, sinking feeling. Whatever he had come to say, it wasn't good news, she thought.

"We would like to speak with Vancy," said the Leader. "It is a matter of some urgency."

"But ..." Lisbet started to protest.

Vancy put a hand on her foster mother's arm. "I won't be long," she muttered, slipping out the door.

She followed the Leader down the street. It was so quiet in the village, she could hear the swish-swish of his robes as he walked. Soft lights from lanterns shone in some of the houses. The children would be tucked up safe in their beds, exhausted after the party.

They passed Kerei's house on the right. A lamp was shining in their front room and Vancy wished that she was inside with Kerei and his parents, chatting about the party, thinking about what they'd do tomorrow. Instead, she was being led to the Council. A matter of urgency . . . It must be important. The Council never met at night. And what could it have to do with her?

Ahead, the cobbles sloped down towards the stone Keep. High up in the smooth, curved wall, a man, just visible in one of the arrow slits, was keeping watch. Always, they were watching. Vancy shivered. It had been some time since the tyrant Herit had tried to attack them – a party of his men had crept out of the dark like hyenas – but still Bassorah was vigilant. They had held them back then, she thought, just as they would any other time.

The Leader turned down a track that led to the meeting house. Lights shone here, too. He opened the door and they entered the large room. Vancy glanced around at this familiar place where the villagers held their meetings. Only the Council were here now, sitting stiffly in a row. She stood before them: a slim girl – some might say thin – her thick, dark brown hair tied back into a knot with string. There were mauve shadows of fatigue beneath her eyes.

One of the women, the Weaver, stood up. "Vancy," she said, "we have had some news we thought you should hear."

Vancy's mind was racing. What could have happened? But, as the Weaver spoke, telling of the messenger and the implications of his message, a feeling of grim inevitability began to grow inside her and her blood turned to ice. Of course, she thought bitterly. Herit. The father she had found only a few months ago – the father who had wanted to kill her because of a wretched prophecy. How stupid of her to think he would leave her alone. She saw again the dark entrance to the Fortress, the courtyard and the metal cage into which they had locked her.

"And so," the Weaver was saying, "even though the peace in Bassorah will continue to be uncertain, perhaps even more so now, the Council does not wish you to go to Herit. He is a bully and we will not give in to his whims. We are determined to fight him, as always. You may be his birth daughter, but you belong here."

Vancy was stunned. They were putting her ahead of Bassorah's safety? She bowed her head, unable to speak. She wasn't even truly one of the Bassorah people. If anything, she belonged somewhere out in the Hinterland. When she found her voice, it was a voice she barely recognised. "But, wouldn't it be better if I went?" she muttered. "If it meant he would leave us alone?"

Behind the Weaver, the members of the Council exchanged glances. They were saying one thing, thought Vancy, but they were thinking another. And they were afraid. The pause confused her. Would they change their minds, just like that, and send her after all?

The Weaver spoke slowly. "It is true that such a pact with Herit, if kept, could mean peace in our region for many decades to come . . . " Voices murmured behind her, as if this was a topic that had already been debated. "However," she continued, "we do not believe in Herit's promise. We do not believe he has changed for the better. We cannot risk sending you to a place that may well be treacherous."

"Then, wh-why have you told me?" Vancy stammered.

"For your safety," explained the Weaver. "If Herit decides to attack Bassorah, he will be coming for you. You must be prepared. We must all be prepared."

Vancy swallowed. Her throat felt dry and gritty.

"And now, my daughter, go home and sleep easy."

"Thank you," she murmured, hurrying to go.

Even before she had gone out the door, the Council's voices were buzzing softly. "Sleep easy?" a voice whispered. "How can any of us now sleep easy?"

Vancy stumbled back into the house, a jumble of thoughts in her head. Lisbet was sitting on the couch, knitting, obviously waiting up for her, and Vancy sat down next to her. The older woman put aside her knitting and drew her close, an arm around the girl's shoulders. In a rush, Vancy told her foster mother what had been said at the Council meeting.

"I always had a feeling something like this might happen," Lisbet murmured. "Ever since you came back from the Fortress with the news that Herit was your father."

Vancy shrugged. Now that the Council had told her their decision, Herit seemed a long way away – a bad dream that would vanish in the morning. Vancy thought again about all those years when none of them had known about her origins. Now she felt she knew too much.

"Didn't you ever wonder where I had come from?" the girl asked.

"You were a gift," said Lisbet. "We didn't want to know."

"What about the silver dog?"

Lisbet shrugged. "In time, we came to think of the dog as a myth. As something we had perhaps imagined."

Vancy rested her head on Lisbet's shoulder. "Tell me again about how you found me."

"Ah," sighed Lisbet. "It was a very special day." Vancy could tell her foster mother was smiling quietly. "Most of us were down at the fields, working as usual, when we heard a terrible squalling . . ."

"A baby's squall," supplied Vancy, who had heard this story many times before.

"Yes, it was a baby, wrapped in cloth, lying at the edge of the fields . . ."

"And then what?" she asked.

"We saw a silver dog, walking away – it stopped once and looked at us, as if to say, 'This is for you to take care of', and then it was gone." Vancy listened to Lisbet's soft breathing. "We never knew how the dog got into Bassorah, or how it got out . . . it could have been a ghost, but there was the baby, as real as anything."

"Me," said Vancy.

"Yes, you," replied Lisbet. "So tiny, and sucking on a stone." She gave a small chuckle. "Erik and I had no children of our own, so it was decided that we should take on the upbringing of the babe."

"And all that time Herit never knew I existed."

Lisbet pursed her lips. "True, and I don't know why he should be taking an interest now."

Vancy squeezed shut her eyes. She had met Herit only once, and now she saw again his mocking eyes as she huddled, a prisoner in his horrid metal cage. "And yet," she wondered out loud, "could it be that he has changed?"

"Can a hyena change its spots?" asked Lisbet drily. She patted Vancy's knee. "It's been a long day. Let us talk about it further in the morning. Perhaps daylight will give us a new view of the matter."

That night Vancy tossed in her bed, trying in

vain to get comfortable. The down-stuffed mattress that was usually so soft seemed full of lumps, and, when sleep came, it was as if she drifted between sleeping and waking. Images moved in and out of her mind: a silver dog, walking through Bassorah, stately and silent. Bright jellies being crushed underfoot. The faces of the Council, but not as she had seen them tonight. Now they were full of hatred and the Weaver was crying. Then the dog, walking beside her. Her hand, resting on his shoulder, stroked the thick silvery hair.

Vancy woke up. Opening her eyes, she found herself outside: a rock wall, a torch burning at the end of a rocky tunnel. She was in the Pass. Was she still dreaming? Yet she could feel gravel under her bare feet.

A hand fell on her shoulder and she gasped. A face in shadow. Terrified, she tried to run, but the hand gripped her.

"Hush, little one."

Vancy blinked and saw that it was Kerei's mother, Merta. Her usually fierce eyes looked soft in the flickering light. "You've been sleepwalking," the woman murmured, and already, Merta was steering her back towards the Keep, back to safety.

III

The next morning dawned bright and clear. Vancy could hear Lisbet already moving around in the house. Shifting the furniture back, Vancy thought. She should offer to help, but there were the ponies to be seen to and a dozen other jobs. Pausing in the middle of her room, Vancy tried to remember the strange dreams she'd had in the night.

She had found herself in the Pass and Merta had escorted her home. Sleepwalking! She had never done that before. And why the Pass – as if she wanted to go out into the Hinterland? It was puzzling, and it made her feel uneasy. And then there was the meeting with the Council in the middle of the night.

Vancy sighed. They might want to protect her from Herit, but now she would feel responsible if anything happened to Bassorah. Somehow she couldn't face seeing Lisbet and Erik this morning.

She pulled open the wooden shutters in her room and climbed out the window.

Up at the ponies' enclosure, Vancy unhooked a bucket and went to the well to fill it. Then she let herself through the gate in the stone fence and poured a bucket of water into the trough. All of these things were done in a daze, so she didn't hear the hurrying footsteps and the clatter of the gate behind her.

"Hey, Vancy!" It was Kerei. "That was a great party last night." He swung himself up to sit on top of the stone wall, long legs dangling. He was probably trying to keep out of reach of the ponies. They still didn't like him. "My mother said there was a messenger last night, but she wouldn't tell me any more than that."

Vancy glanced up. Kerei's mother was on the Patrol.

"Funny thing is, they've put him up in the Keep." Bassorah didn't get many visitors, but if any came, even a messenger, they would be given a bed in somebody's house.

"Is he still here?"

The boy shrugged and pulled a piece of straw out of his hair. He looked as if he'd been sleeping in the barn. "Dunno. Why?"

The ponies had been drifting out of their dark stalls and into the enclosure and were nudging around Vancy now. Absentmindedly, she held out her hand to pet them and the small, hairy animals stamped their little hooves, butting and shuffling. Kerei lifted his feet up out of reach, just in case. They were spiteful enough to bite him for no good reason.

Abruptly, Vancy came to a decision and let herself out of the gate. "Because, I'd like to see him."

Kerei grinned. "Really?" When somebody new arrived at Bassorah, people were always interested in where they had come from. He hopped down from the fence. "Let's go, then."

As they walked down the cobbled street that ran between the houses, Vancy thought about the man she was hoping to see. Chances are, thought Vancy, he would have been guarded last night, because he had come from Herit.

"Will your mother be at the Keep?" Vancy asked.

"Nope, she was up all night. With a bit of luck," he added with a grin, "she'll be asleep. Safely out of the way, while we have a chat to our guest."

At the bottom of the slope was the stone Keep, standing opposite the natural tunnel known as the Pass, guarding the only way in or out of Bassorah. It was a tall, circular building of rough-hewn blocks, with narrow window openings that looked out across the Hinterland.

They went around the side of the Keep to its only door. It was dim and cool inside. Two men were sitting at the table in the central room, drinking mugs of coffee. One of them was dressed in the black leather jerkin that marked him out as Herit's man. The other was a member of the Patrol. A pack lay on the floor next to Herit's messenger.

"Hey up, you two," said the Bassorah man in greeting.

"Has the Council given its return message yet?" asked Vancy.

"That's what we're waiting for."

She nodded. "Could we, um, speak with the messenger?"

The Bassorah man got up from the table. "Be my guest. Though whether he'll speak back to you is another story." He went over to a basin to rinse his mug.

Herit's man watched from under beetled brows as Vancy stepped forward. She wasn't sure exactly what she wanted to know. "I . . . I am Herit's daughter," she said. Although he made no reply, a light of recognition came into the man's eyes. Vancy took a deep breath.

Now what? She summoned up her courage. "I would like to hear the message," she said.

The man hesitated, as if about to refuse but, after glancing again at Vancy, he seemed to change his mind. He got to his feet, straightened his back and lifted his chin. "I wish for my blood daughter, Vancy, to be returned to me," he announced, knocking his fist against his chest for emphasis. "She shall be Princess Regent and, on my death, shall inherit my lands. In exchange, I shall leave the fine people of Bassorah in peace. If, however, you do not look favourably upon my request, then I shall take my daughter by force. The choice is yours, Bassorah. This I proclaim!"

The man sat back down at the table and picked up his mug of coffee.

"Crivets," breathed Kerei.

Vancy sat down opposite the man. "Can you tell me, will Herit keep his promise, about Bassorah?" The man's dark eyes slid away from her. "Please," said Vancy, "I need to know."

The man reluctantly met her gaze. "I am instructed to speak no more than the message, miss," he said in a low voice, as if he might be overheard. And he bowed his head over his mug.

It was obvious she would get no more information

out of the man. She left the Keep, with Kerei hurrying after her.

When she got back to the house, Tem was out in the rear courtyard talking to Erik. One of the Council had taken Kerei away: as part of the Watch, it was his job to let the whole community know there would be a meeting that evening. They both knew what that would be about. With a sigh, Vancy watched him race away.

"Ah, Vancy," said Tem, as the two men stepped into the house. "This is terrible news."

She shrugged. "The Council doesn't seem too worried."

Erik and Tem exchanged glances, as if they disagreed. They had obviously been talking about the message. "Tem had come over to say goodbye," Erik explained. "He was going to go back to his village."

Vancy's heart sank. She had known that her uncle wouldn't stay in Bassorah forever, but she had hoped he might stay a few months longer. Especially now.

"Except this isn't the time to go," Tem added quickly, as if reading her mind. "I will stay and see what happens with Herit." He was looking at her with sympathy. Vancy had not known her birth mother, but she had often wondered if her mother had also had Tem's kind brown eyes.

"There's no point," she said miserably. "Nothing might happen, and then you'd be waiting for no reason."

"But still . . ."

Erik put a hand on Tem's arm. "Vancy's right. You are ready to go home. Herit might yet leave us alone."

"It has been a long time since I last saw my village," murmured Tem. "In fact, fifteen years. They might not even recognise me," he added, trying to make a joke of it. The mood in the room, however, remained heavy.

"Well then," said Erik heartily, "you must stick to your plans."

"When are you going?" asked Vancy.

"Tomorrow, at dawn."

Vancy sat in a dark corner of the meeting house, her knees drawn up to her chin. Above her the stained beams that held up the thatch roof were lit up by the lanterns. Nearly all of the adults in the community were squeezed into the house and sitting on the straw-littered floor, listening to the

Leader of the Council. He had stated the situation and the Council's thoughts; next there might be a debate. If you had something to say, you stood up and spoke, then sat down again. Important issues were sometimes debated all night, with all sides given a hearing. Vancy had sat in on several such meetings, but usually slipped out before they were finished. She didn't have the patience for it.

This time, however, was different. This time the Council had already made its decision.

After the Leader had spoken, a heavy silence fell and one or two people looked around to find Vancy. She pressed herself further into the corner. Tension mounted in the room as nobody rose to speak, and nobody even moved. Heads turned as one woman left the house, slipping quickly out the door. Her footsteps, clattering up the cobbled slope, sounded clearly in the hushed room.

Why didn't anybody speak! Vancy could hardly stand it. She wanted to shake somebody.

Finally, an old man struggled stiffly to his feet with the aid of his carved stick. A sigh ran through the room.

"We respect the decision of the Council," he said. Then he, too, started for the door. People moved their knees and feet to clear a path for him.

Next Della, who tended the chickens and geese, stood up. "Yes, we do respect the decision of the Council, of course. But will we be safe?"

Murmurs rose up from the assembly. Then, one by one, people began to stand up and speak. Vancy listened with growing anxiety as she heard their fears, especially those of the older folk, who remembered earlier assaults Herit had made on Bassorah. How long could they hold him back, they asked. Now that Bassorah finally had a chance to be at peace with Herit, the Council had decided not to accept that peace. That was what it came down to, she thought bitterly, and people would blame *her*, not the Council. She alone had the power to make things right. And, if she didn't, how would she live with herself? How could she even keep on living in Bassorah? If Herit attacked them – if people got hurt – *she* would be blamed, and hated for it.

The voices faded out as Vancy hung her head in self-pity, bitter tears falling onto her knees.

Then she heard her name. "Let Vancy speak," a voice called.

The girl swiped at the tears on her cheeks and rose shakily to her feet. All heads turned towards her, and her face burned. Vancy had never spoken at a meeting before. Lisbet and Erik, sitting against the far wall, were watching her with bated breath.

"I . . . I have met Herit," she began in a quiet voice.

"Speak up," somebody cried.

Vancy raised her head and gave a little cough. "I have met Herit and I know that he will not let something alone. If I do not go, then he will do as he says, and come to get me . . . " She broke off, her mouth dry, trying to get her thoughts into order. "And I don't think that would be very good for Bassorah." Murmuring voices raced across the room. "We have been lucky before, but maybe this time will be different." More voices, louder now.

"Please," said the Leader, "no interruptions until the speaker has finished." The room fell quiet again.

Vancy glanced over the expectant, upturned faces. These were people she'd known all her life: her family, her community; people who had taken care of her and given her a home. How could she let them down now? And yet, she wished that messenger had never come to Bassorah. She wished that things could have just gone on as normal. Now it was too late for that. Everything had changed.

"So, I have decided to go to the Fortress . . . "

The room erupted with voices. "Order, order," cried the Leader, but no-one listened. Everybody was talking at once. The Leader was rapping his stick on the ground. "Order, please . . . "

Vancy, in dismay, slipped out into the night and ran up the hill to her house.

In the dark before dawn, a single bird was calling – *scritch scritch scritch* – from somewhere out in the Hinterland. Vancy, waiting in the puddle of light cast by the torch that burned every night above the Pass, tried to locate the bird, but it was too dark out there to see anything.

She had spent a restless night, worrying about her decision. Late, after midnight, she had heard Lisbet and Erik come quietly into the house. She heard their whispered voices as they paused at the doorway of her room, before carrying on to their own room. So the debate had gone on a long time. All the more reason, thought Vancy, for simply going, before people tried to convince her to stay. That was, if they did. Maybe they wanted her to go. Maybe that was why the debate had gone on for so long. In the meantime, Vancy had packed her things. Let them debate; she was going to leave with Tem at dawn.

If he was still going, she thought now. What if,

after the meeting, he'd changed his mind?

Vancy kicked idly at a rock, sending it skipping off into the darkness. Then she would just have to go by herself. Except that idea made her shiver. She wasn't as brave as *that*.

Footsteps sounded behind her and she whirled towards them.

"Vancy!" cried Tem, jumping back a little in fright.

"I'm leaving with you," she told him, shouldering her pack, "but I'm going to the Fortress."

A sad look came into her uncle's face. "You don't have to do this," he murmured. "People will understand . . . "

Vancy shrugged. "Maybe."

Tem shifted his own pack on his shoulders, making himself more comfortable under its weight. "All right then, if you're sure?"

"I'm sure," she said firmly, though in fact, Vancy felt far from sure.

"Then I'll travel with you towards the Fortress and then cut across the mountains. I'd go all the way with you, but you know Herit would probably kill me. He holds a grudge for a long time."

Vancy nodded. Herit would have blamed Tem for the avalanche that nearly destroyed the Fortress.

With Kerei and Squirt's help, she and Tem had tried to destroy Herit – make his wretched prophecy come true – and if only they had!

"If you change your mind," her uncle continued, "you can come with me to visit my village. Does that sound reasonable?"

"Yes," she said, "thanks."

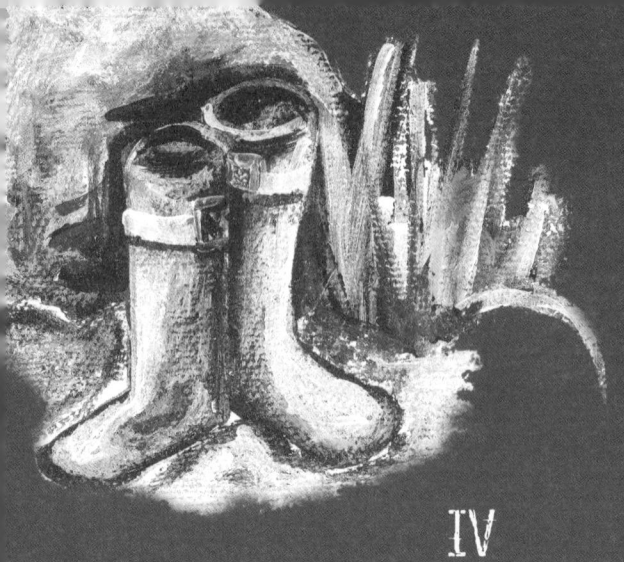

IV

Squirt was in the Keep, sitting near the men at the long wooden table, when Kerei burst in. "There you are! I've been looking everywhere for you." It had been a frustrating morning – he'd searched for his friend up in the fields, then at the little lake over the ridge, before remembering Squirt's new job at the Keep.

Squirt frowned and shook his head at Kerei.

"What?" the boy exclaimed, shoving onto the bench next to Squirt. "*What?*"

As the ginger-haired boy put a finger to his lips, the men, who had fallen silent when Kerei burst in, resumed their conversation. Their voices were serious and muted. Something about wild dogs.

Kerei didn't have time for this kind of boring talk. Squirt might think he was in training for the Keep, but this was much more important. He nudged

Squirt in the ribs. "Come *on*," he hissed urgently. "Outside!"

Squirt rolled his eyes, but he followed his friend out into the sunlight, where Kerei was already talking a mile a minute. " . . . and then I went along to her house to tell her about the meeting and Lisbet said . . . then Erik was talking to me . . . Turns out that . . . "

"Kerei, slow down," cried Squirt, wiping at his face. "I can't make out a thing you're saying. And you're spitting. I hate it when you spit."

Kerei took a deep breath and squared his shoulders. "Vancy," he said carefully, "has already gone."

"What? Gone where?" asked Squirt impatiently. It was obvious his mind was on the Keep and whatever discussion was going on in there.

Kerei released an exaggerated sigh. "She's already gone, with Tem, off into the Hinterland."

His friend frowned. Kerei had his full attention at last. "She's gone to the Fortress?"

Abandoning any pretence of patience, Kerei grabbed Squirt's arm and started dragging him up the street. "Yes, yes. Where else? Come *on*! There's no time. We have to get packing and follow them."

"Kerei, listen . . . " began Squirt.

But Kerei was in no mood to listen. He dragged

his friend into his house, interrupting his mother and father, who were obviously in the middle of a serious discussion, judging by Merta's expression. "Don't mind us," said Kerei, hustling Squirt through the living area towards the side corridor that led to his room.

As soon as the boys reached Kerei's room, an urgent, whispered debate started up. With luck their voices wouldn't carry through to Kerei's parents in the other room.

"Look, it's not like last time . . . "

"I don't care. She doesn't know what she's getting herself into. We can't just let . . . "

"But we've seen the Fortress. There'd be nothing we could do."

"So you're going to just leave her to walk into his evil clutches . . . "

"There's no need to be sarcastic."

"I wasn't being sarcastic. I was being honest."

"I don't think . . . "

The boys were interrupted by Kerei's father, who poked his head around the door, a quizzical expression on his kindly face. "Hello, you two," he said. "Not up in the fields today, Yager?"

Squirt, looking embarrassed, cleared his throat. He hated his real name. "Um, no. I've been assigned to the Keep now. I'm supposed to be in training," he added pointedly, glaring at Kerei.

"Oh, good." Kerei's father didn't seem to notice that the boys looked as if they were about to hit each other. "I've just made a jug of lemonade. Would you like some?"

"Yes please," Kerei answered quickly. He waited until he could hear his father moving around in the kitchen area, then pulled out the pack he had hidden under his bed and went back to his frantic packing. "We'll need extra rations – we didn't take enough food last time – and . . . "

"Stop saying 'we'. *I'm* not going."

Kerei looked up with a startled expression on his face, as if Squirt had said something rude. It was soon replaced by an angry frown. "You call yourself her *friend*," he said in an accusing voice.

Squirt looked at his hands. "I *am* her friend."

"Well then!"

"Well nothing. It's different this time."

Kerei shoved a shirt into the pack. "Yeah, last time it was *you* who wanted to go to the Hinterland," he said quietly, "and maybe it wasn't about Vancy at all." He thought back to the day Vancy had vanished, running away into the Hinterland to find her real parents. Then it had been Kerei who was scared and didn't want to go, and Squirt who had convinced him they were doing the right thing in following her. It seemed an age ago now, even though it was only a few months.

"Just shut up about that." Squirt jumped up from the bed, his fists clenched. "It wasn't just about going into the Hinterland."

Kerei stood facing his old friend. They'd known each other since they were babies playing in the red dirt at the edge of the fields. If it came to blows, then so be it. Kerei was determined to go after Vancy, whether Squirt came with him or not. "Then what's your problem this time?"

"I just don't think we should interfere this time." Squirt's face was pale. "We should trust Vancy. She has chosen to go."

"Look," said Kerei, his dark eyes serious, "I think she's walking into a trap. And she's so stubborn, she'd go anyway, no matter what the Council said. Well I, for one, am going to stop her."

"She knows what she's doing," hissed Squirt.

A voice called from the other room. "Lemonade's ready."

Kerei made for the door. "Come and have a drink," he said over his shoulder.

But Squirt pushed past him and left the house.

In the kitchen area, Kerei's father had poured out two mugs of lemonade. "What's got into Yager?" he asked, still looking in the direction of the slammed door.

"I dunno," shrugged Kerei, reaching for one of the mugs. "Are those potato cakes?"

By nightfall, Vancy's feet were very sore. She sat on a low boulder and peeled off her boots to rub her feet. Already, blisters had sprouted on her reddened heels. "There must be a better way to travel than this," she complained.

"There is," said Tem, "only Bassorah doesn't have them."

"You mean by greathorse?"

Her uncle nodded as he laid his bedroll. "Yes, like the ones Herit has. Much faster than walking."

Vancy dug in her pack for an apple and took the little knife from her belt pouch. Carefully, she cut the fruit into quarters and started on the first piece. She had eaten hardly anything all day and now she was hungry.

"Bassorah people have never been much for travelling around," she said between mouthfuls.

Tem shrugged. "Perhaps it's safer that way."

The girl's eyes gleamed in the fading light. "I'd like to travel, to see everything," she said.

"And perhaps one day you shall," said Tem with an affectionate smile.

Vancy glanced up sharply. "What is it?" asked Tem, suddenly alert.

"I heard something," she said in a low voice.

"Well, there are animals out here," he muttered, gazing into the dim light. The sky was grey with cloud and it was getting darker by the second.

Vancy hugged herself. "I'd like a fire, if you don't mind?"

"Yes, good idea," said Tem. He was bending again to his pack when Vancy cried out sharply. Around them, dog-like shapes were emerging from the gloom. Vancy saw drooling fangs, spotted haunches, lowered heads. A pack of hyenas.

"Oh dear," breathed Tem. "Don't make any sudden movements."

Vancy turned the blade of the fruit knife, still clutched in her hand, so that it pointed down, ready to stab. "Will they attack us?" she whispered.

"Depends," murmured Tem, "on how hungry they are."

Slowly – ever so slowly – he lowered himself to the ground. His hand snaked out towards a large rock.

The hyenas prowled, getting closer, surrounding them, coming in for the kill. *Now I know what it feels like to be a rabbit*, thought Vancy, tightening her grip on the knife.

"Whatever you do, don't turn and run," Tem muttered.

Slowly, he drew back his arm. Then, with a sudden movement, he hurled the rock at the largest hyena, hitting it with deadly aim right between the eyes. The hyena yelped and fell back, tumbling head over heels. Then it leapt to its feet, turned and ran. After a moment, the others followed.

Vancy drew a ragged breath. Her hands were shaking. Tem, who looked as if he was shaking, too, came over to give her a quick hug.

"Now," he said, "I think you were talking about a fire . . . "

V

They took turns keeping an uneasy watch through the night, but the hyenas did not come back. Sitting on a rock in the dark, a blaze of stars overhead, Vancy shuddered to think of how she had crossed the Hinterland alone – not so long ago. She had been so headstrong. So ignorant. It was a wonder she'd survived at all.

By the time the sun was high and hot, Tem and Vancy were walking across the barren reaches of the Hinterland. The mountain range on their right was ash-blue – not much snow up there this time of year. Vancy was wearing a scarf over her head to keep the sun off her face.

"Just as well there was all that food left over from the party," Tem was saying. "Should be enough to keep us going over the mountains. Once we're on the other side, I can always catch the odd rabbit."

"You talk as if I'll be there, too," said Vancy, frowning at him.

He glanced across at her. "I'm still hoping you will be," he said quietly.

They had been walking for a few hours now and Bassorah was already far behind them. Glancing back, Vancy could barely make out the grey smudge of its cliffs. She sighed and looked ahead into the emptiness of the Hinterland, which seemed to go on forever. But she knew it didn't. Somewhere up ahead was Herit's Fortress.

"Do you think he'll keep his word?" she asked, thinking about Herit and Bassorah.

"He might, I suppose," replied Tem. "Perhaps he has turned his gaze elsewhere."

"There isn't much else out here, except the silver dogs."

Tem smiled. "Ah, the dogs. How I'd love to see them again. Perhaps I'll go that way, before heading south."

Vancy wondered how the dogs were faring, and whether she would ever see them again, either. Perhaps, one day, she would find the secret tunnels that ran under the mountains on the eastern side of the Fortress and visit the dogs. If she was allowed to leave the Fortress.

"Tem," asked Vancy, "do you think I will be a prisoner there?"

Her uncle shook his head. "I've no more idea than you have, Vancy. But, if Herit is serious about your being his regent, then you must surely have some kind of freedom. How much freedom will depend on Herit's will."

Vancy shuddered as she remembered the metal cage outside the Fortress, and Herit's rasping voice. *Tomorrow, at dawn, you will once more be left in the desert.* His eyes had been like stones. His look had made her feel like a mouse, about to be eaten by a bird of prey.

She tried to imagine what it would be like to live at the Fortress. There must be some kind people there, she reasoned – ordinary folk who could look after her. But how kindly would they be when they realised that it was her who had tried to destroy the Fortress by avalanche? In her mind's eye, she saw the Fortress as it had looked from so far above: the avalanche as it crashed down towards it, the explosion as the snow hit the furnaces.

"I still don't understand why he wants me there. What about the prophecy?"

"Perhaps he thought," muttered Tem, "that the prophecy was over and done with, once we had sent down the avalanche. Because, in a way, we did destroy him. Just not permanently enough," he added in a bitter voice. He put a hand on her shoulder. "You can send a message to me," he said, "if you need help. You could send one of the dogs. I have a feeling they won't be far away."

Vancy nodded, not feeling any better. Even if she wanted to send a message, and if she could find one of the dogs, Tem's village was still several days' walk from the Fortress. It would be quicker to send one of the dogs back to Bassorah. But she kept her thoughts to herself. Her uncle meant well. Only she wished now that she had stayed in Bassorah.

"You shouldn't be doing this alone," Tem muttered.

The girl squinted into the distance. The horizon was hazy white with heat. "It's better this way," she said feebly, struggling to believe it.

Kerei was on his knees, eye to eye with one of the mill ponies, holding a rope out to one side. He had the littler stinker hypnotised, he was sure of it. Now all he had to do was get the rope over its head – very slowly, so it wouldn't bolt. The other ponies were watching this procedure with much interest from the back of the enclosure.

"Stea-dy," Kerei muttered between his teeth. "Near-ly there . . ."

One of the other ponies let out a high-pitched whinny and Kerei's pony, which had been as still as a rock, jerked up its head. Then it whirled around and aimed a swift little kick at Kerei's head. He just had time to fling himself off to one side as the hoof sailed past his face and clipped his arm.

"Owww!" he cried as he landed in a patch of manure, cursing loudly.

The sound of laughter burst from the stone wall and Kerei, clutching his arm, found himself glaring up at Squirt's upside-down face.

"I'd get out of there," said Squirt in an unhurried tone, "if I were you."

Kerei glanced back at the ponies. They were clattering madly around the enclosure. Any minute now they would trample him into the ground. He leapt up, forgetting all about his sore arm, and vaulted over the wall.

"That was close," he panted as he collapsed onto the grass next to Squirt.

"Yeah. Those cute little ponies would have eaten you for breakfast."

"Cute!" snorted Kerei. "You sound like Vancy."

At the mention of the girl's name they both fell silent. Kerei examined his sore arm and Squirt plucked a piece of grass and started shredding it.

"You weren't seriously trying to catch one of those ponies, were you?" asked Squirt eventually.

Kerei sniffed. "That's none of your business, seeing as you aren't coming with me." He hadn't yet noticed the other pack propped next to his against the wall.

"Well," said Squirt thoughtfully, "I still remember being bucked off that wretched pony we took out into the Hinterland."

"Have you got any better ideas?" snapped Kerei.

"Actually, yes, I have," said Squirt, getting up. He grinned as Kerei noticed the pack and broke into a delighted smile.

"I knew you'd change your mind!"

"Yeah, right."

"So what's this brilliant idea?" asked Kerei. "It had better be good. It'll take ages to catch up with them. They've already been gone for hours."

"Oh, don't worry, we'll catch up," said Squirt with a cunning look.

"Yes?"

"Yep. Come with me. I've got something to show you."

"Crivets!" breathed Kerei. "What, by the gods, is that?"

"Um, I'm not too sure. The men think it might be some kind of horse."

The boys were staring at a grey-haired beast, peacefully cropping the grass in a fenced area behind the Keep. Long, slender legs made it much taller than the mill ponies. Now its ears were twitching at the sound of their voices and it turned to watch them, a mournful expression on its long, bony face.

"The Patrol found it wandering out in the Hinterland, so they brought it back. Nobody's decided what to do with it yet."

"And you think we can ride this thing?"

Squirt put his head on one side. "Don't see why not."

"It looks friendly enough," allowed Kerei. He held out his hand. No sudden biting lunge – always a good sign.

"I think it *is* friendly. The men just brought it back with a rope," said Squirt. "Though maybe that was because it was hungry and thirsty. It's spent the last two days eating."

The boys gazed thoughtfully at the beast. It gazed thoughtfully back at them.

"It doesn't look very comfortable," said Kerei, looking at its narrow spine. The ponies, at least, had broad little backs, so they weren't too bad to ride, even if your feet were nearly touching the ground.

"We could tie a blanket round its middle."

"A mattress, more like," snorted Kerei.

"Well, have you got any better ideas?"

"Um, not right at this moment."

"All right then," said Squirt. "I'll go and fetch a blanket and some rope."

VI

On their second day of walking, a dark blotch appeared on the distant horizon. Vancy, squinting towards the east, could barely make it out. Throughout the day, the blotch slowly grew in size until it took on a recognisable shape: the dark bulk of the Fortress, brooding in the barren landscape like a nightmare. Glancing at Tem, Vancy could see her own anxiety reflected on his face. They had fallen silent long ago, thinking of all that lay before them.

"It doesn't look any different from here," she said, thinking about the avalanche that had seemed to destroy half the Fortress.

"No, they've been busy," agreed Tem. "Doesn't look as if they've repaired the metal furnaces though."

No smoke, thought Vancy.

"At least we put him out of action for a little while," muttered Tem.

They had stopped for a rest among some tussock plants and a cluster of small rocks. A yellow lizard flicked across a rock and out of sight.

Tem began to pull food from his pack. "What do you want to eat?" he asked.

"I'm not hungry," said Vancy, her eyes drawn to that dark shape in the distance.

"You've got to keep your strength up."

To keep Tem happy, Vancy took an apple, but she felt sick to her stomach with fear. What kind of life was waiting for her in that place of stone and metal? Still, it wasn't too late: she could go with Tem, travel to his village and forget all about Herit. Yes, and one day go back to Bassorah to find it destroyed. A tear slipped down her cheek and quickly she swiped it away. No mother. A tyrant for a father. Her life seemed particularly ill-fated.

She looked up to find Tem watching her thoughtfully. "It's not far now to the place where I will cross the mountains," he said quietly. "Have you changed your mind?"

Vancy pictured herself travelling with Tem, visiting the dogs, seeing his village for the first time ... the village where the mother she had never met had grown up. Then she thought about Lisbet and Erik and all the people back home. They'd be at the mercy of Herit's fury. There was no choice, she thought bitterly.

"I have to go on."

And so she arrived: a slight figure, footsore and weary, walking alone up to the Fortress and the stone gates in the high outer wall. It was late in the evening and the sun was beginning to sink in the west. The outer walls loomed above her – a sheer face of stone blocks. It was a place built for defence, thought Vancy. To keep people out.

Through the gates she could see a large paved area and steps leading up to a yawning black entrance way. The doors stood open, as if the place was waiting for her. *I ought to be afraid*, she thought, but there was only a numb feeling where the fear should have been.

A guard sprang to attention. "Halt!"

Obediently, Vancy stopped.

Now the man was observing her closely, his eyes widening with surprise. Yes, it was a girl, and she appeared to be alone. "State your business," he demanded uneasily.

"I've come from Bassorah," said Vancy. "Herit wants to see me."

At the mention of Herit's name, and that of Bassorah, the guard made a fist and struck his left breast. "Follow me," he barked and strode off across the open, paved area, with Vancy jogging to keep up with him.

As she went, Vancy took in as much of her surroundings as she could. Off to the left was a large, half-built chimney – they were obviously rebuilding the furnaces. There was the place where the cage had once stood. It was gone now, probably swept away in the avalanche. The outer wall over that side was still broken and stones lay in unruly heaps. Vancy followed the guard up the steps until he came to a halt at the doors. "Enter," he told her, standing back and motioning her to pass.

Vancy eased the pack off her aching shoulders and, carrying it at her side, stepped into a huge hall. Thick candles burned at the far end, their flames guttering in the breeze. It was so big! She could hardly see the ceiling. Vancy had never been in such a large place. When she had been here before she hadn't seen inside the Fortress. The size was staggering. She wished Erik could see this room.

Then she noticed the people. Something was

going on. They were gathered, their backs turned to her, at the far end of the hall, where a deep, low voice was speaking – giving a speech by the sound of it. Echoes ran around the room. Perhaps they were having a community meeting? Vancy made her way around the back of the group. She could smell food now and realised she was hungry.

"Um, excuse me," she asked, lightly tugging at the sleeve of the short, thin man nearest her. "What's going on here?"

The man glanced at her, then jumped back in fright to make way for her, tapping his neighbour on the shoulder as he went. That person – a grey-faced woman – also gasped in fright and got out of the way.

"Anybody'd think I was cursed," Vancy muttered to herself.

As the crowd parted around her, Vancy soon found herself at the front of the group where a man in a long brown robe sat in a large chair on a raised platform, his eyes half-closed in thought as his voice rose and fell. He had the authority of a leader: his short-cropped hair, streaked with silver, gleamed in the candlelight and he wore a band of silver around his forehead. A hundred candles burned around and behind him. The rumble of his voice was the only sound to be heard in this great hall, despite the many people, including children, gathered there. Not one of them coughed or made any sound. A bit different to Bassorah's Council meetings, thought Vancy, where people were always coming and going and asking questions.

It was Herit.

"We will rule all of these lands," he was saying. "I am your father and I shall provide . . . Too long we have been small – now is the time to grow, to expand, to claim what should be ours. The ghosts of our forebears will rise up, and we will be mighty . . ."

Suddenly, his eyes flicked open and, glittering in the flickering light, came to rest on Vancy. The rumbling bass voice stopped in mid-sentence and his gaze fixed on her like a snake on its prey.

"Ah, she has come!" He stood and stepped forward to meet her. Vancy felt a lurch of fear, but stood her ground. "Despite the message from Bassorah, here she is. My daughter! Welcome." He glanced around him, taking in the people, the mighty hall. "Welcome to my humble abode."

Now he turned slightly to address the silent crowd once more. "My people," his voice boomed, "welcome your new regent."

A murmur ran through the crowd and a slow clapping started up, echoing off the stone walls. The sound chilled Vancy. It was a defeated sound, far from welcoming. Wan faces stared at her. Children hid at the edges of the crowd, cowering behind their mothers' skirts. Old men leaned on sticks. There was something about these people, but Vancy couldn't put her finger on it. A feeling came from them. But what? Hatred? Hatred of her because she was from Bassorah? A young, dark-haired woman, standing off to one side, was staring at Vancy with hard eyes.

She looked away quickly to find Herit's gaze on her, a faint smile on his lips.

"Have you come here of your own free will?" he asked. Vancy nodded, unable to speak. "Excellent," he exclaimed. "From now on, this shall be your home."

Yes, she thought, *my home*, his words burrowing into her mind. Although later she would struggle to remember exactly what he had said.

"You must be tired . . . daughter," said Herit in a silken tone. It was as if he were trying out the word on his tongue, to see whether it pleased him or not. Again, Vancy was reminded of the cage, and of the menace behind those eyes. The moment came and went in a second.

"And how dusty you look." Herit smiled thinly. "That will be taken care of." He gestured to the dark-haired woman, who stepped forward, her black eyes fixed on Vancy. Another younger woman followed her. They both wore long, dark dresses and silver bands around their foreheads.

"Yes, master?"

"Take the Princess to her room."

Vancy followed the two women through the crowd, which moved back quickly to make way, and crossed the hall towards a dim corridor that seemed to be carved out of the rock itself. Despite her exhaustion and anxiety, Vancy couldn't help but be fascinated. So different to Bassorah! Every now and then, she saw carvings in the rock walls, and hollows where lanterns burned. They passed doorways – some lit to reveal cave-like rooms filled with mattresses, others in darkness. Vancy trailed her fingers along one of the walls, feeling the pitted surface of the rock.

"Um, is this a natural tunnel," asked Vancy, "or man-made?"

The dark-haired woman in front held her small lantern higher as she glanced back over her shoulder, but said nothing. Perhaps they spoke another language? Vancy quickened her steps to catch the woman closer to her. "What's your name?" she asked her.

The woman in front stopped abruptly as the others came up behind her. "Her name is Agate, and I am Mica."

Agate had moved to stand behind Mica once more, but she looked much friendlier than the other and even offered Vancy a timid smile. "The Fortress is built on stone," she murmured. "This passageway was here long before we came."

They were climbing now, going up a long flight of shallow steps. Slit window openings appeared in the left-hand wall as the passage curved to the right; they must be climbing into the higher part of the Fortress. Now there was a sloping, almost level stretch, then more steps.

Suddenly, Mica stopped and held up her hand. In a moment, Vancy could see why. There was a huge hole in the wall on her left. Below, she could just make out the dim courtyard. Scaffolding was fixed against the wall. Their avalanche had made a mess all right, she thought grimly.

Holding up her lantern, Mica was picking her way around a pile of rock. Vancy followed, just as carefully. She didn't want to slip and fall through that hole. It was a long way down to the ground.

At last, they turned through a doorway. In the room beyond, a narrow bed stood below a narrow window opening, through which a cool breeze was blowing. On a small wooden table stood a jug and a folded cloth. For a moment, the younger woman, Agate, looked as if she was going to say something, but Mica laid a warning hand on her arm.

"You will stay in this room," Mica told her.

Then, without a word or backward glance, they left Vancy alone, taking the light with them.

She stood looking at the empty doorway for some time, half hoping the women might reappear and tell her what to do next. Slowly, her eyes grew used to the dark, assisted by a beam of moonlight coming in through the window opening.

She sat down on the bed and found it hard, as if made of stone, covered only by a thin mattress stuffed with straw – Vancy could feel it prickling under her hands. The breeze had risen a little, sighing into the room with a lonesome sound. She would have cried, but she was too exhausted. A dark veil was slipping over her mind. Slowly, Vancy leaned sideways and down until she had curled herself into a ball on the bed. Everything went black.

VII

"Squirt?"

Jog jog jog. "Yeah, what?"

"Do we know – *jog jog jog* – how to stop this thing?" *Jog jog jog.*

"How should *I* know!"

The landscape was going past at a steady, trotting rate. Kerei, who was clinging to the beast's mane and trying not to slide off between its very long ears, couldn't feel his knees any more. True, his knees were still clinging to the sides of the beast, but they seemed to have gone numb. Squirt was hanging on to Kerei's back with one hand and gripping the rope with his other.

For the first hour after leaving Bassorah, the boys had been very pleased with their progress. This was certainly a more pliant animal than the mill ponies; they had managed to climb on to it without getting bitten or kicked and it had set off quite happily. It soon settled into a good even pace and for the first hour they had been in fine spirits. The journey was off to an excellent start and, at this rate, it wouldn't take long at all to catch up with Vancy and Tem.

There was only one problem. The beast didn't seem to want to stop, and, without a bridle or reins, the boys had no way of controlling it.

"Cause what I'd really like to do," said Kerei between gritted teeth, "is stop and have a little snack. Maybe stretch my legs, um, and, you know . . . "

"Yeah," agreed Squirt. "Me, too."

"All right then," decided Kerei. He addressed the beast: "Whoa!" he cried.

The beast flicked its long, soft ears and kept trotting.

"Whoa there!" cried Kerei again, this time adding a kick for good measure.

There was a soft whinny and a little break in the rhythm of the trotting.

"I don't think you should have done that," muttered Squirt.

"Why not? It's not a mill pony. It's not going to buck us off. This is a friendly, helpful beast."

"No, but I just have a bad feeling that . . . "

He didn't get to finish his sentence because he was holding on for his life. The beast had kicked up into a faster speed. They were cantering now, not trotting.

"Ye gods . . . " Kerei's voice fell behind on the breeze.

The beast was not only cantering now, it had also turned at a right angle and was heading for the mountains, as if the Dread Lizard was at its heels.

"Turn it back to the east," cried Squirt.

"I can't," gasped Kerei, clinging to the beast's neck. "I'm going to fall off."

"No you're not," said Squirt. "If *you* fall off, *I'll* fall off, and I am *not* falling off!"

Kerei swallowed as rocks and tussock plants rocketed past beneath the hooves of the beast. Best not to look. He squeezed his eyes shut. He was dimly aware that Squirt was clinging to his back. Look on the bright side: this couldn't go on for too long. The thing would wear itself out. No animal could have the stamina to keep going this fast. Just had to hang on . . .

"Uh-oh," said a voice behind him.

Kerei opened his eyes and yelled.

"Huh!" Vancy cried out, sitting bolt upright. *Where was she?*

She glanced around wildly – a strange room. Sounds she didn't know. Hammering. Neighing. Grey, rock walls. A sharp pain in her neck. And so hungry!

Then she took a deep breath and swung her feet to the cold floor. Somebody had taken off her boots during the night, although there was no sign of them. The Fortress. She was in a room in the Fortress. She got up stiffly from the bed, rubbing her sore neck, and peered out the window opening. Barren land stretched away as far as she could see. It was morning; the sun had barely crept up into the sky.

She patted herself down, feeling grimy after the journey and looked around her. The jug on the table held water and she used the cloth next to it to wet and wipe her face, then her arms. There was something new on the bed: a long grey dress. *Hmpf.* If they thought she was going to wear that, they had another thing coming.

She would change into her spare shirt instead, but when Vancy looked around for her pack it was gone. Out of all her things, only the hairbrush remained, placed beside the jug of water.

Then she heard footsteps. It was Mica and Agate, looking more relaxed by the light of day.

"Hello," said Vancy.

Mica nodded and stepped into the room. "Master says you must wear our clothes," she said, pointing at the dress on the bed.

"Master?" said Vancy sarcastically. She was hungry enough to eat a hyena and wasn't in a mood to be mucked around. "You mean my father, Herit. Well, you can tell him I don't wear dresses."

Mica's face had flushed and she looked ready to retort when Agate stepped forward. She had long dark hair, braided down her back, and wore a plain dress like the one on the bed. In the morning light, they all had a chance to examine each other more closely. Vancy thought the two young women looked similar enough to be sisters.

"What's it really like in . . . Bassorah?" asked Agate.

"Don't," said Mica. "It's just about the dress." Agate cowered back against the doorway, as if she'd been slapped. "You must wear our clothes," said Mica, more firmly this time. "The Master has said."

Vancy frowned. "Or else what?"

"Or else I will put it on you myself," hissed Mica.

"Sister," murmured Agate, touching her arm.

Mica shook her off, glaring at Vancy.

"Where are my clothes?"

"You don't need them here," said Mica. "We burned them."

More than anything else that had happened so far, that shook Vancy. A visitor to Bassorah would never have been treated so rudely. "Even my scarf?" Lisbet had knitted that scarf for her a year ago – grey-green, with a special ivy leaf pattern. Burned? She looked at the two young women in dismay. Agate couldn't meet her eye.

"The dress," insisted Mica.

Vancy shrugged. If they were going to get upset about it, she might as well try the thing on. She lifted up the dress by its shoulders. It didn't look too bad. At least it was plain. "I've never worn a dress before."

There was a giggle, and then Agate slapped a hand over her mouth.

Vancy gave them both a questioning look, but neither woman moved. "Um," she said, "I will want to put it on?"

Mica nodded, understanding that Vancy wanted privacy. "We will wait."

They went out of the room and a little way along the corridor. Vancy could hear their whispered conversation as she quickly peeled off her own crumpled clothes and slid the dress over her head. It rustled into place, fitting her perfectly. She smoothed it down. Not *too* bad, she supposed. But if Kerei or Squirt ever saw her in it she would kill them. She tied her belt around her waist and looked around for her boots.

Mica was standing in the doorway again, holding out a pair of shoes. They were made of a fine leather, dyed black, with a pointed toe. Vancy turned them over in her hands. "Not all that good for walking," she muttered, "or for anything much else." She caught Agate's eye. The young woman was watching her closely, as if holding her breath. Vancy shrugged and dropped the shoes to the ground, sliding a foot into each one.

Agate, at least, seemed happier now. Mica signalled for her to follow them.

This time, in the light of day, Vancy took careful note of their route. She would want to learn her way around this place, so that, when the time was right, she could . . . escape? She didn't know yet, but she was determined not to stay in this stony place forever. It would never be her "home".

They stepped carefully around the rocky hole in the wall – that would be tricky to navigate quickly in the dark, thought Vancy. Down below, men were busy working with mallets. Some of them were working on the scaffold against the Fortress wall. Others were carrying baskets of stones back and forth across the courtyard. A greathorse was being led by a man. Horses! She had only ever seen one up close, and that hadn't been in ideal circumstances. She was itching to find out more about them.

"The horses," she asked. "Do you ride them?"

Mica, who was once more walking ahead, snorted, as if it was beneath her to answer such a stupid question.

"Oh, yes," said Agate eagerly. "Out in the Hinterland."

The tunnel curved its way down and eventually opened on to the great hall. It, too, looked different in the daylight – more cheerful somehow. The mighty doors were open and sunlight was streaming in over some long tables where people were eating breakfast, by the look of it. No sign of Herit, Vancy noticed with relief.

Mica gestured for her to take a place at a bench. The sisters sat on either side of her. A little child on the other side of the bench, spoon poised in mid-air, was staring at Vancy with an open mouth.

"Good way to catch flies," commented Vancy.

The child promptly dropped the spoon into the bowl and ran off crying.

There was a pause. "Just a joke," she muttered. The night's rest had brought back some of the old Vancy – the one who wasn't silently afraid. All she needed now was some food and she'd feel much more herself.

A bowl had appeared in front of her and now all thoughts of the strange Fortress ways and the days ahead were banished as she tucked into the steaming bowl of porridge and honey.

The sheer side of a mountain rose directly in front of them – at least, it looked sheer – and the beast was cantering straight towards it. They were going to slam into a mountain and be turned into pancakes.

"Whoaaa!" screamed Kerei.

The beast took absolutely no notice. It was impossible to guess what was going through its small brain, but it began barrelling straight up the side of the mountain, rocks flying back down the slope behind them. Kerei, who had shut his eyes, cautiously opened them. He was still on the beast and Squirt was still hanging on behind him. At least the thing had slowed down now. It could only walk up the mountain, not canter. Kerei sat up and looked back over his shoulder. The Hinterland was spread out behind them like a giant grey-brown tablecloth. He cleared his throat.

"Well, that was fun," he said drily.

"I still want to get off," muttered Squirt. "I can't feel my backside."

"If this, erm, thing wants to climb up the side of a mountain with us on its back, then I say we should definitely let it. Besides, I don't think I can walk."

They had reached a light smattering of snow now, and still the beast kept on. Before long they had reached a plateau, and the beast pricked up its ears at the sound of trickling water. A spring was bubbling up from between rocks, forming a small pool. The animal stopped at last, lowered its head and sucked deeply at the water.

The boys, as if glued together, slid off the beast and crumpled to the ground as one.

"My legs," moaned Kerei.

"My bum," groaned Squirt.

The beast gurgled on.

Kerei sat up, rubbing some life back into his numb legs. "Where are we?"

Squirt looked around. "Not far from Tem's old place." A low building was just visible in the distance.

"And that means . . ."

"That we're fairly close to the Fortress," Squirt said grimly.

VIII

"And everybody lives inside this place?" Vancy asked in amazement.

Mica nodded. "It has always been this way."

After breakfast, they had taken their bowls into a kitchen area on the right-hand side of the great hall. Embers burned in a long fireplace, where blackened pots hung in a line. A long bench, carved out of stone, ran along the opposite wall and served as a working area. Women and boys were busy there, chopping, mixing, kneading. Others, along the far end of the room, were wiping dishes. They had jugs of water and basins over which they worked. A smell of baking bread filled the room.

Vancy picked up a knife lying on the bench and felt its edge. Metal. Her own little knife was made of stone – chipped and polished to a fine edge. But this knife . . . Vancy sighed as Mica firmly took it out of her hands and put it back on the bench.

They went back out into the hall. "We have chores now," explained Agate.

"You will work with us," added Mica.

That wasn't exactly what Vancy had in mind. She also wasn't very keen on spending the day with her two guards – for that was what they seemed to be. Assigned to keep an eye on her. "Could I use your, um, bathroom first?"

"Come with me," said Mica. "I will show you."

Vancy followed her out of the hall and back up the corridor they had come down earlier. They went past two rooms, then entered a third. This one actually had a curtain across the doorway. Inside the dim room was a long, low bench carved out of stone. At regular intervals there were holes in the stone where a person might sit. Hmm, thought Vancy, communal toilets. They certainly did things differently in this place. She really hoped this room was just for girls.

"I shall wait for you back in the hall," murmured Mica, leaving Vancy alone.

The girl counted to ten, then twitched back the curtain. The corridor was empty. Good. Quickly, she turned right and headed back up the corridor, as if making for her room. There were some steps they had passed that she wanted to explore. This place had to have back doors, she reasoned. The steps weren't very far along the corridor, and went down through a cutting in the wall on her left. Holding up her skirt so she wouldn't trip, Vancy ran down the steps.

Yep, just as she'd thought: a wooden door that pushed open to reveal the outside of the Fortress and a cool grey day. She stepped out into the paved yard and looked around. There was the half-finished furnace chimney. Another stone chimney lay on its side, where it would have broken away from the furnaces, near a gaping hole in the paving. People were also busy working on the damaged outer wall of the Fortress.

Vancy started off around to the right, following the wall of the mighty building towards a sound of whinnying. As she rounded a corner, a stone wall appeared with a large, open grassy space beyond it. There were vegetable plots, a few stunted trees and animals. Despite all she had been through and the strange circumstances she found herself in, Vancy smiled. She had found the horses.

In a shelter similar to the one that housed the Bassorah ponies, Vancy stood petting and talking to a huge piebald horse. It was quiet and steady, as if patiently waiting for something. How different from the nervy mill ponies. Every now and then, it pulled a mouthful of straw from the pallet. Its brown gaze watched her without curiosity.

"He's a beauty, en't he?" A man no taller than herself was leaning against the shelter's frame.

"Oh yes," said Vancy. "He's lovely."

"His name's Nubby. Least, that's what I calls him."

"Do you look after the horses?"

"Aye," he said, coming forward to rub the side of Nubby's neck. The horse nibbled his hair. "I be the groom around here, and stable boy and whatever else is needed. Here," he added, handing her a bundle of freshly washed carrots. "Give him this. You'll be friends for life."

One by one, Vancy fed the carrots to the horse and the stall was filled with the sound of his enthusiastic crunching. "Is this the only horse you have here?"

The man chuckled. "Nay. Master's out on his today. Another two have gone off trading. And I've got a mare about to give birth in a separate enclosure."

"Oh," breathed Vancy, "I should like to see a foal."

"I daresay you shall," he said. After a pause, he

added, "You're the Princess, en't you?"

Vancy flushed at the unfamiliar word. "Um, not exactly," she muttered.

"Must be a bit strange for you, eh, being in this place?"

"It *is* a bit different from home," she admitted.

"Well, you can always come down here, if you want some company," said the man.

Moved by the man's kindness, Vancy ducked her head to hide the tears that pricked at her eyes. She fed the last of the carrots to Nubby, blinking rapidly. "He's so big. Does he stay in this stall all the time?"

"Lor, no," said the man. "I takes him out every day for his exercise. In fact, I was just about to do that next." He took a bridle and set of reins from a hook and slipped them over Nubby's head, rubbing the horse's ears as he did so. "He likes his run out on the plains. He could go all day if I let him."

Vancy walked beside the man as he led the horse out into the yard. "But how do you get up on him? Do you climb on a box or something?"

The man laughed. "Nay, miss. I'll show you how I get up on him." The groom took hold of the horse's mane and, with a quick spring, jumped up onto his bare back. Nubby stamped his front hoof, eager to be off. "Steady," he said to the horse, adjusting the reins in his hands. "Would you be kind enough, miss, to open the gate for us?"

"Of course," she said, walking over to open the gate in the wall.

"Uh-oh," said the man cheerfully, "here comes trouble." Mica and Agate were hurrying around the corner of the Fortress. "I'll be off then," he murmured, walking the horse past the two women and towards the main gates.

Leading the beast by its rope, the two boys walked the rocky track that ran along the mountain ridge. They had taken the horse's blanket off and were using the rope as a lead. Far below, they could see the dark smudge of the Fortress. Ant-like people were moving around down there, and a thin line of smoke rose into the sky.

"Do you think she's in there already?" murmured Kerei.

"Don't know," answered Squirt, "and I don't know how we'd find out, either." He stared at the dark building below, frowning. "We need to figure out a plan."

"I thought we'd just, you know, sneak in there

after dark and find her and then get her to come back to Bassorah with us."

"Hmm, let me see," muttered Squirt. "We sneak in past the guards and all that . . . then we, oh yes, just happen to find Vancy straight away, without getting caught by anybody . . . then she'll just agree to come along back with us to Bassorah. Great plan."

"Well, you think of something better then," huffed Kerei.

Squirt kicked at a stone, sending it bouncing down the slope on their left. Behind him, the beast ambled along, occasionally nibbling at his backpack.

"You can't, can you?" crowed Kerei.

"Give me time. I will!"

"Yeah, right."

The boys fell silent. Now that they were out here, so close to Herit's Fortress, Kerei was starting to see the hopelessness of the task ahead. It was stupid to have rushed off like that, without getting some kind of help. They could have persuaded one of the Patrol to come with them, but then, Kerei knew what they would have said. Vancy was going of her own free will, for the good of Bassorah. And he knew Squirt was right: even if they did manage to find her down there, without getting captured, how were they going to persuade her to come back with them? Vancy could be as stubborn as one of her ponies, and just as prickly.

Kerei's reverie was broken when he realised Squirt had been saying something. "What'd you say?" Kerei asked him.

"I *said*, let's go and see the silver dogs before we do anything stupid. They might be able to help. Besides, we can go through their tunnel and come out on the other side of the Fortress. Might be less obvious that way."

Kerei brightened at the thought of seeing the dogs again. "Now you're talking."

They had reached the building crouched on the ridge line. It was Tem's old place, where he had lived for all those years with his goats, watching over the Fortress below. It was empty now. The boys were tempted to go inside and camp for the night, but a quiet sense of urgency pushed them on. They took the track leading away from the building – a track that meandered down from the ridge line and headed towards the golden plains below, on the other side of the mountains.

Mica and Agate were hurrying towards her – Agate pale and agitated, but Mica plainly furious. When they reached her they each took one of Vancy's elbows and gently but firmly guided her out of the horse enclosure.

"You must stay with us," murmured Agate. "We are your sisters now."

"You must stay with us," echoed Mica, more stiffly than her sister, "or you might get hurt." The tone of her voice told Vancy that Mica was serious. But hurt by whom? And why?

Vancy shrugged them off. "All right, all right," she said impatiently. It was like being a prisoner. "I was just looking around. No harm done."

The sisters regarded her silently. Clearly they didn't agree.

Over by a long chicken coop, two men were also staring at Vancy with open curiosity. When she caught their eyes, they looked away. No word was spoken, no smile exchanged. So different from Bassorah, where the people were always chatty and friendly. Vancy felt a pang of homesickness. There was a heavy, brooding atmosphere here that she didn't like. It was probably something to do with that great big stone Fortress, she thought, looking up at its towering walls. It looked even more gloomy and monstrous during the day than it did at night. And up there somewhere was her little room – *cell*, more like, she huffed to herself. What did they think she was going to do, run away? She had made a deal and she was sticking to it . . . at least for now.

They had walked around the other side of the Fortress now, where smoke was coming from a tall chimney that Vancy supposed was above the kitchen. Here another wooden door opened into yet another dim corridor. Vancy took careful note of where they were going, counting the door openings on the right of the corridor. Many rooms, bedding on floors, glimpses of neatly folded piles of clothing, cloaks hung on hooks.

"What's this?" she asked, pausing at a narrow flight of steps that led down into darkness.

Agate gasped faintly and hurried on, but Mica, who was in the rear, shoved Vancy forward. What was her problem? It was obvious they didn't want her to know what was at the bottom of those steps. Never mind, thought Vancy, she'd find out sooner or later. In the meantime, she needed to get hold of some candles, or a little lantern. She would need some light if she wanted to explore the Fortress.

They came out again into the great hall, where people were working at the long tables.

"Chores?" asked Vancy.

Mica nodded and showed her to a seat.

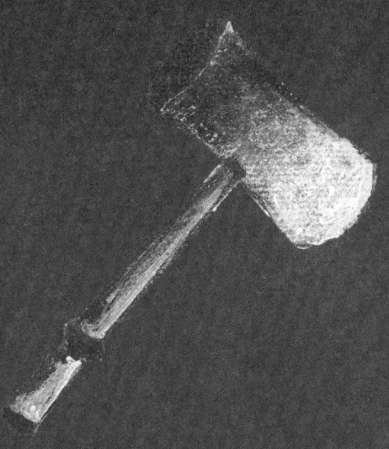

IX

If only she could put a door between herself and the rest of the Fortress! A good solid door with a good strong lock, but no, there was only the door opening and beyond it the dark corridor. Moonlight shone through the window opening in her room, throwing a thin white line across the stone floor. A bird called outside – a high, haunting sound that made her jump.

Vancy sat in the bed, holding her knees tightly clasped to her chest. Sleep was far away. If only she was back home in her own nice warm bed, in her own nice house with Lisbet and Erik sleeping in the next room. She had never felt so homesick as she did now. Why had she come to this horrible place where everybody seemed to hate her?

She lay down miserably, trying to make herself comfortable. Bits of straw stuck into her. The pillow was hard as rock, and every sound made her nerves stretch tighter. Was that the sound of stealthy footsteps coming along the corridor? She stared at the doorway, holding her breath. Mica was coming with a knife of steel to stab her – Vancy was sure of it!

A mouse skittered past, pausing for a moment in the open doorway to clean its whiskers.

Vancy pulled her own little knife out of her pouch, which was still tied around her waist. There was no way she was going to be parted from her last precious possessions. Everything else had disappeared. She had no idea where her pack had gone, and her old clothes had also mysteriously vanished.

The girl lay curled on her side, tightly clutching the knife, eyes fixed on the doorway. Just let them come! She was ready. Even if it meant she had to stay awake all night.

She blinked. No, she wasn't imagining it. There was a suggestion of light, if you could call it that – a silvery light that just licked at the doorway. Oh no, somebody really *was* coming to harm her . . . somebody with a lantern. But they were so silent – she hadn't heard a sound. She should sit up . . . No, better to stay lying down, as if she were asleep. That way, they'd be fooled into thinking she was asleep.

She'd have more of an opportunity. She held her knife more tightly, ready to stab.

Still there was no sound of footsteps, no stealthy movement, no dark figure in the doorway. Yet the light was growing. A soft, silvery light. Vancy's eyes widened in amazement. The light was forming itself into a shape. Quickly she sat up. There in the doorway stood a silver dog, its long, soft coat ruffling in a breeze she couldn't feel. How had it got up here?

But no, it wasn't a real dog. It was . . . she didn't know *what* it was. A ghost?

The silver dog was looking sadly at her. *Vancy . . .* She could hear it speak her name.

"Wh-where are you?" she whispered. "Dog? Are you nearby?"

The dog seemed to bow his head a little. Vancy hugged herself. It was the same dog she had met all those months ago. The leader of the silver dogs. The dog who had left her, as a baby, at Bassorah. But, why didn't he "speak" to her? She knew he could communicate. Yet the dog just stood staring, as if watching something in the distance.

"What are you trying to tell me?" Vancy murmured.

The dog was shimmering now, his edges starting to melt.

"Wait," she cried, kneeling and reaching out for the dog. "Don't go!"

Now the light was fading, fading, until there was just the dark, empty doorway once more. She waited, breathless, but the dog didn't reappear. All was silent and still. Vancy curled up again in the bed. Her heart felt like stone. "Don't leave me here alone," she whispered.

"Tem!" cried Kerei. "What are you doing here?"

The older man came forward to greet them, smiling a welcome. "I might ask you the same thing."

After a day's walking along a dirt track fringed by tall grass, they had reached the cave of the dogs, only to find Tem sitting on a rock under a tree. Beyond him stretched a vast plain of long golden grass, dotted with trees.

Kerei dropped his pack on the ground. "You said you were going back to your village . . . "

"True," said Tem, "but I thought I'd visit my old friends again." His face clouded. "And just as well I did, too."

Squirt was tying the beast to the tree. "What do you mean?"

"I'll tell you later," Tem muttered, "but first tell me what you two are doing out here."

The boys looked at each other guiltily. "We, um, have come to rescue Vancy."

Tem chuckled. "I don't know if she needs rescuing this time, boys."

"We'll be the judge of that," said Kerei sulkily. "Once we find her."

Tem held up his hands. "Don't worry, I won't interfere with your plan."

"If we *had* a plan," muttered Squirt under his breath.

"Except," added Tem darkly, "it would not be a good idea to go to the Fortress. You know that. Not unless you're invited."

The boys exchanged a look. "So Vancy's already inside?"

Tem nodded. "She's a determined young woman."

"Stubborn, more like," said Kerei. More and more, he was thinking he should have stayed at home. His plan seemed more pointless than ever.

Tem was examining the beast. "And where did you find this mule?"

"Mule?"

"Yes, it's a cross between a donkey and a horse."

"Donkey?"

"Er, yes. Sort of like one of your mill ponies, but with much longer ears."

"Ah," said Kerei, looking around to avoid Squirt's eye. "Where are the dogs, anyway?" he asked. Usually, there would be dogs lolling around outside the cave, enjoying the late afternoon sun, or coming back through the long grass from hunting. Now there was only a deep silence.

Tem shook his head sadly. "They're in the cave," he said, "having what we might call a meeting."

"What's going on?" asked Squirt, flopping onto the grass.

"Well, it's an odd story," replied Tem, resuming his seat on the rock. "You see . . . " He stopped, his attention caught by something over their heads.

A large silver-haired dog was walking towards them. Behind him, other dogs were appearing from the cave: stretching, looking around, coming over to sniff the new visitors. A pup, all legs and nose, bounded over to trip on Squirt's legs. The boy grinned with delight as another pup latched on to the end of Kerei's boot.

"Hey, let go," he said, shaking it off.

The large male dog – obviously the leader of the pack – sat down near Tem and looked at the boys. His fine hair was as silver as ash and his grey eyes gleamed with intelligence. Even though Kerei had seen the silver dogs before, he still stared in awe. He was aware of a murmur in his head – the many voices of the dogs – and images of running and hunting and lolling in the sun. Then Kerei realised there was something else as well: a shadow in the minds of the dogs.

"I think he's pleased to see us," whispered Kerei.

"I'm getting that feeling, too," said Squirt.

A picture was forming in Kerei's mind of Vancy, sitting on a rock talking to the silver dog. It was from the time when they were last here. He glanced quickly at Squirt, who nodded back at him.

"He wants to know where Vancy is," said Squirt.

"Well, how do I tell him?"

"Make a picture in your mind of the Fortress – of Vancy going there."

Kerei sighed. "I'll try, but I'm no good at this kind of thing." He closed his eyes and concentrated. The silver dog looked puzzled, his head on one side. "It's no good. I keep thinking about roasted potatoes."

Squirt frowned and took over. "Herit wanted her," he explained to the dog. "She travelled across the Hinterland," he said, seeing the girl clearly in his mind as he spoke, "to the Fortress."

The boys studied the dog to see if he had

understood. The dog looked from one to the other of them, as if for confirmation, and his expression was one of deep sorrow. He had understood.

"There's something else," said Kerei. As if somebody were telling him a story, a picture came into Kerei's mind. He frowned, trying to understand what it was. A field of mounds and stones? He pressed his hands against his eyes, trying to see the image more clearly. The dog's silvery ears flicked towards them, then lay back. Another picture formed in Kerei's mind, this time of an old dog lying curled in a shallow hole. Another dog was covering the old dog with dirt.

"What's he trying to tell us?" Squirt asked Tem.

Tem shook his head, indicating they should keep "listening".

And then . . . a dark figure . . . Kerei couldn't make it out properly . . . a man, digging among the stones?

A yelp came from behind them and the silver dog looked up. A bundle of pups was rolling on the ground, fighting. The dog stood up and walked over to the pups, separating them with his snout. Just then, another dog appeared from the long grass, carrying a dead rabbit in its mouth, and dropped it at Tem's feet.

"Ah," said Kerei. "Dinner." He got up, dusting himself off. "I believe this calls for a fire."

Squirt fingered the rabbit's fur; it was still warm. "What's happening, Tem?"

"They have a problem," said the older man, "with their graveyard."

"The dogs have a graveyard?" the boy asked in surprise.

"Oh yes. It's quite ancient. The very first dogs are buried there. They don't have any predators out here, you see, on this side of the mountains, so they mostly die of old age. When an old dog knows its time is getting close, it goes to the graveyard with a younger dog – a sort of companion, I think." Tem paused, watching Kerei collecting stones and twigs to make a fire on the flat space in front of the cave entrance. "The younger dog digs a hole and the older dog curls up in it and dies. Then the younger dog covers him up."

"That's what he was showing us."

"Yes."

"So, what's the problem?"

They were interrupted by Kerei. "Are you going to skin that rabbit, or keep it as a pet?"

Squirt started to get his knife out of his pack, but as he did so he glanced up at Tem, who was watching him with dark eyes. "What's been going on, Tem?"

"Somebody," he answered quietly, "has been stealing the skulls of the dogs."

Two days passed before Vancy saw Herit again. The evening meal was being prepared in the kitchen and she was washing turnips in a bucket of water when Mica appeared at her elbow, in a way that Vancy was beginning to find unnerving. "The Master wants to see you," Mica said in a low voice. A chill ran through Vancy as she dropped the turnip back into the bucket of water and put down the brush. She wiped her hands on the dress (it had its uses, after all) and followed Mica out of the kitchen.

They crossed the great hall, where an old woman was setting out metal platters. Vancy, who had been wondering where Herit's quarters would be, expected to go into one of the two corridors that ran off from either side of the hall. Instead, Mica led her out of the main entrance way. Vancy blinked in the evening light. She hadn't been allowed outside since she had found the horses. The sky was painted mauve and pink with the setting sun, but she didn't have time to admire the scenery. Mica was hurrying around the Fortress to the left.

They came to a narrow door standing open in the Fortress wall. Inside, a large room seemed to be carved out of the stone itself. Vancy looked around, amazed. This room must be underneath the hall. She wondered what other rooms and secret passageways might be hidden away beneath the Fortress.

"As you can see," said a voice, "the Fortress has many secrets."

Herit stepped forward, out of the shadows. His greying hair was clipped close to his skull; a narrow window in the stone cast a sliver of light across his face, turning his eyes black. Vancy looked nervously around for Mica, but the young woman had vanished. She was alone with Herit – her father.

He gestured for her to have a seat. There was a table with a platter of food on it and two metal plates. Two chairs were pulled up to it. Vancy sat, her mouth dry. She couldn't imagine being able to eat anything. Herit settled himself opposite her.

"It is ancient, too," he continued. "It was here long before we discovered it."

He picked up a knife, fingering its sharp blade thoughtfully, then speared a piece of roasted meat. His fingernails were long and pearly. As if remembering his manners, he gestured for Vancy to eat. Gingerly, she chose something that looked like a vegetable and nibbled on it. It was bitter, though its nutty flavour was pleasant enough.

"My ancestors . . . " he began, then corrected himself with a thin smile. "*Our* ancestors did not come from this area. We were nomads originally, until we found this place." He waved the knife in the air, indicating the Fortress. "It was smaller then, and empty. We never learned what had taken place here to leave it uninhabited, but it didn't matter. Over the years, first my father, and then myself – we have made the Fortress into the stronghold you see today."

Vancy watched as he speared another piece of meat and put it in his mouth.

"Bassorah, too, must have a similar history," he said, eyeing her keenly.

"Maybe," she said, taking another vegetable. She didn't know what sort of meat he was eating and she didn't want to try it. So far the only animals she had seen were chickens, horses and a kind of stocky pony with long ears.

"Of course," continued Herit smoothly, "they are not your people, so perhaps you aren't so very interested in the history of Bassorah." She tried to think of something to say, but he didn't seem to expect her to answer. "But, over time, Bassorah, too, has built itself into a stronghold. Wouldn't you say?"

His eyes never left her face and Vancy squirmed under his gaze.

"Why am I a prisoner here?" she asked bluntly, hoping to change the subject.

Herit gave a dry laugh. "But, my daughter, you are no prisoner. You are free to leave at any time." The expression in his eyes made a lie of this statement. "Do you wish to leave?"

Vancy took a sip of water to avoid his gaze. "No," she said.

"Well then, there is no problem," said Herit cheerily. "And do you like your new dress?"

"Um, it's all right."

Herit was pouring wine into his cup. "The cloth comes from a village to the east, four days' ride away by horse. We trade with them to obtain items we ourselves cannot make." Herit drained the cup and eyed Vancy. "Perhaps Bassorah would like to trade with us? My people would enjoy some fish from their lake."

"I don't know," Vancy muttered. "You'd have to ask the Council yourself."

"Ah," sighed Herit. "So there *is* a lake. I thought it was simply a legend."

Vancy started and blushed. She had walked right into his little trap.

"Fortunate Bassorah," Herit continued, as if unaware of her discomfort, "with its plentiful supply of water and its protected fertile valley." Then he laughed, as if the subject meant nothing to him. "However, I am being rude, my daughter. Please have some wine."

But Vancy was pushing away from the table now. "I'm tired," she said quickly. "I'd like to go back to my room."

Herit, too, stood up. "Of course, of course." He clapped his hands and Mica appeared at the door, as if by magic. She must have been waiting outside the whole time. She would have heard Vancy making a fool of herself.

She hurried out of the room, following Mica back to the main entrance. As she crossed the great hall, aware of the people gathering there for their evening meal, Vancy bowed her head, avoiding the stares she must be attracting. She felt as if everybody was staring at her. Had she just betrayed Bassorah? But surely it would be common knowledge that they had a lake? Yet it seemed that Herit hadn't known that – he was only guessing. Was that the real reason why he wanted her here? To act as a spy and divulge all Bassorah's secrets?

Deep in thought, she didn't notice that Mica had

stopped and walked right into her. There was still enough light for Vancy to see the glittering look of hatred in the young woman's eyes. "You might be his daughter," hissed Mica, her face very close to Vancy's, "but I am his *true* daughter." It sounded like a curse. "*I* am the one who matters to him. Not some little upstart from Bassorah," she spat.

Vancy took a step backwards and lost her balance on the uneven floor. As she stumbled, Mica swiftly caught her by the elbow – a painful hold.

"We may be sisters in blood," she hissed, "but he hates you – the one who tried to destroy him. Just as the prophecy foretold."

Then Mica released her, turned on her heel and went marching back the way they had come.

Vancy leaned against the rough wall and took a deep, shuddering breath. She was surrounded by enemies. Exhausted, she carried on up the sloping corridor in the rapidly fading light, towards her solitary room.

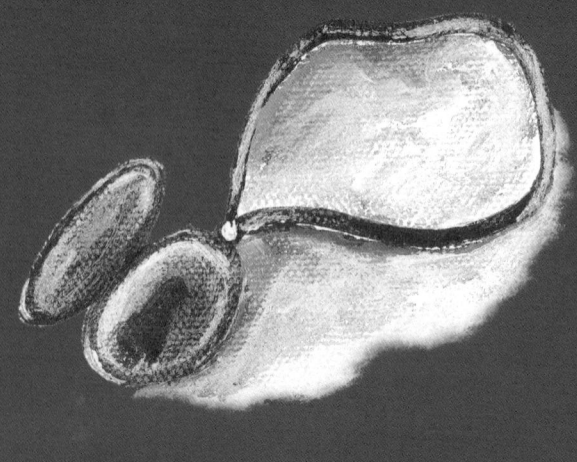

X

"M'lady?"

It was a timid, mouse-like voice. Vancy, who had excused herself from the repetitive, boring "chores" by pleading a headache, was lying on her bed. She raised herself up on an elbow and saw a small, elderly woman, standing in the doorway.

"M'lady, am I disturbing you?"

Vancy sat up. "Please don't call me that. My name is Vancy."

"And I am Onyx." The woman ducked her head and crept into the room. "I saw you had left the great hall, so I made bold to come and speak with you." Her face was lined, with a gentle expression. Apart from the horse man, hers was the friendliest face Vancy had seen in the Fortress. Thinking back, she remembered glimpsing this woman among the others, watching her. Vancy patted the bed beside her and the woman, bowing and scraping, came to perch on its edge.

"I was your mother's servant," she said modestly.

Vancy's heart leapt. "My mother – really?" She knew her mother had lived here for a time, but nobody had yet mentioned her name. It was as if she had never existed. She had died soon after giving birth to Vancy. Tem, her brother, had brought her to this Fortress to marry Herit. It was supposed to make a union between their village and the Fortress.

The woman was wringing her tiny, age-spotted hands. "She was so lovely. I miss her every day."

Vancy had so many questions, but where to start? "What did she look like?"

"Why," the old woman said with a smile, her eyes grazing over Vancy's face, "just like yourself, miss."

Vancy found this hard to believe. Like her, with her tangled, unruly hair and lanky limbs? She had always imagined her mother to be elegant and regal – not at all like herself.

Onyx took Vancy's hand and stroked it. It was a bit embarrassing, but she didn't like to pull away. "She was so young. Yet brave, too. To come from such a faraway place and make herself a new home here, which must have been so different."

So she and her mother had that in common at

least. Vancy could imagine her mother's loneliness for green fields and laughter. The Fortress was so barren and inhospitable.

"And then she had her little babe – you." The old woman's face clouded.

"And what happened to that babe?" Vancy asked carefully.

Onyx bowed her head. "At the time, we thought she went to the angels."

So she didn't know the truth, thought Vancy – that Herit had left her, as a baby, to die out in the Hinterland. It was only because of the silver dog that she had survived at all.

"But look now," continued Onyx. "Here you are – a miracle."

"I didn't know about my mother," breathed Vancy, "until a few months ago. I don't suppose . . . " She hesitated, not knowing what exactly she wanted to ask of this woman. "I don't suppose there are any mementoes of her?"

The old woman also hesitated. Then she ducked a hand into the front of her dress and pulled out a locket strung on a piece of leather. She opened the locket and showed it to Vancy. Inside, etched on polished metal, was the tiny image of a young woman with long, flowing hair. Vancy touched her own thick hair, now tied back into a manageable knot.

"That's her?" she whispered.

Onyx nodded. "She brought light and joy to our community. It hasn't been the same since she . . . left us."

"But," protested Vancy, appalled by the old woman's sorrow, "that was fifteen years ago. If you missed her so much, you could travel over the mountains to visit her village."

"How could I do that?" Onyx looked shocked. "The Master can protect us here. Out there, there is only the Hinterland – or the plains over the mountains, where your mother came from. If I left the Fortress, I would be devoured by wolves."

"I have been in the Hinterland," said Vancy, "and I haven't seen any wolves."

The woman's eyes widened in disbelief. "But there are terrible wolves. The Master has told us. One of them would rip a poor woman like me to shreds in a moment."

"Well," Vancy conceded, feeling uncomfortable with the direction the conversation had taken, "it's true there are hyenas . . . "

"And wolves," insisted the old woman, like a child frightened by shadows. "Wolves as big as a donkey!"

"A what?"

Just then they heard a bell ringing faintly – the signal that kitchen duty was about to start. Onyx jumped up. "But I must not tarry. The Master would not like it if he knew I was speaking with you." And, before Vancy could say anything more, she had scurried off.

Vancy was still puzzling over the strange conversation, and Onyx's obvious fear, when footsteps sounded in the stone corridor and Mica appeared in the doorway. She sniffed suspiciously at the air. "Has somebody been up here?" she asked with narrowed eyes.

"No," said Vancy. "Only me."

"It is time for our kitchen duties," said Mica, turning on her heel.

And what a bundle of fun that will be, thought Vancy, reluctantly following her.

When they reached the great hall, Vancy noticed several people standing at the doors, whispering and looking into the distance. Out in the Hinterland, a large silver dog was sitting on its haunches, staring at the Fortress. Vancy felt a thrill of relief at the sight. So the dogs weren't far away after all.

One of the guards picked up a stone and hurled it at the dog, but it simply moved out of range.

"Vermin," muttered Mica, looking out at the dog. Then to Vancy and the others: "Get back to your chores."

They stood at the edge of the dusty field and looked at the stones. If each stone represented a dog, then there were many dogs buried here. Pictures came into their minds of dog ancestors: running, playing, sitting curled in the big cave with the rest of the pack. The silver dog stood silently, giving them time to examine the graveyard. Then he stepped forward, walking with great dignity around the areas marked with stones. Now and then, he would pause and indicate the graves where digging had taken place.

"But what would you do with a dog's skull?" Kerei whispered to Tem.

"I cannot imagine," he said. His arms folded and his gaze on the silver dog, Tem seemed lost in thought.

Kerei nudged Squirt, hoping to get more reaction out of him. "Who do you think's doing it?"

Squirt was frowning, his gaze also following the dog around the field of graves. "There's only one man in this region who would do something like this."

"Herit?"

"Who else?"

"But why?"

Squirt shrugged irritably. "How should I know!" He began to walk away, back to the cave, with Kerei in pursuit. "I have a bad feeling about this," he panted, hoping Squirt would stop and talk to him about it. "I mean, he makes Vancy go to the Fortress, and now we find out about this, er, dog thing. What if they're connected?"

Squirt stopped and rubbed a hand through his hair. "Why did she go?" he muttered. "We could have protected Bassorah . . . we have in the past. Why did they let her go?" He glared at Kerei, who raised his hands in innocence.

"Look, it's not *my* fault. I'm not on the Council. Besides, they didn't know she was just going to go off like that."

"She's so headstrong," huffed Squirt, but whether it was from anger or admiration it was hard to say. He kicked at a stone. "I just wish . . . "

"What?"

"Nothing." He looked up as Tem and the silver dog caught up with them.

Back at the cave, they sat in a circle with the dog leader. The rest of the pack were lolling and dozing in the sun at the front of the cave. Other, older dogs had already headed out through the long golden grass to hunt. They were waiting for the silver dog to tell them what was happening, or give them some clue as to how they could help.

"What's he trying to tell us?" muttered Kerei to Squirt.

Confusing images were flashing through his mind. There was a man digging. A silver dog rising up from the ground. *No* – the ghost of a silver dog rising up. A man wearing a dog's skull on top of his head. The same man standing on a rock, the skull on his head, and raising his fist to the sky. Silvery dogs moving through the night. No, being pulled through the night – against their will. The ghost of a dog looking back over its shoulder, wanting to go back, but being pulled forward.

And then . . . Kerei heard a gasp, which he thought came from Tem. Or it could have been himself, he couldn't tell. Images were whirling through his head. He saw the cliffs of Bassorah. The Keep. And then . . . and then? He could barely make it out. Something moving across the Hinterland – a large grey force, like a cloud being blown across the land by the wind. Heading towards Bassorah. *What was it?*

Ghosts. The ghosts of dogs. An army of ghost dogs descending upon Bassorah.

Kerei's eyes flew open.

Kerei, Squirt and Tem stared at each other in horror.

Dreaming. But it was a dream so vivid it seemed real. Vancy was walking beside the silver dog and he was showing her a field of stones. *But what is this place?* she asked him. She expected the dog to show her a picture of his thoughts – the way he usually communicated – but, instead, he spoke in clear words.

The ghosts of our forebears will rise up, said the dog, *and we will be mighty.*

In her dream, Vancy was puzzled. What did he mean, and where had she heard those words before?

The dog was looking out over the field of stones. Something was happening out there. Vancy felt a twinge of fear. *This is only a dream,* she thought. *It can't hurt me.* A dog was rising up out of the earth. Huge as a tree, it kept coming out of the ground. Then she saw – Vancy started to scream – that it had no head.

There was a lull in the afternoons when there seemed to be some free time. Children ran outside, old people chatted and dozed on benches set up in the sun. Onyx sat in a quiet corner of the hall, knitting. Vancy was just thinking about slipping away to her room when Mica appeared carrying two swords, making for the main doors.

"Come on," said Agate, who was never far away. "Let's go and watch Mica's sword practice."

She took Vancy's hand and together they went down the steps to the wide, paved area. Mica had signalled to a young man working on the broken furnace chimneys to come forward and take one of the swords from her.

"We can watch from over here," said Agate.

They sat on a bench against the Fortress wall as Mica and the young man faced each other, tapped swords and began fencing. The sky was studded with puffy white clouds and the mountains loomed overhead. Tem's old house, thought Vancy, would be just up there. She thought of him walking through the great golden plains towards his home village. She must have cousins there – her mother's people.

" . . . of the Fortress," Agate was saying.

"Excuse me?" asked Vancy.

"I said, the sword practice will be useful," Agate

repeated patiently, "for when she is ruler of the Fortress."

Vancy glanced at Agate's pale features. That was a surprise: according to Herit's "invitation", it was Vancy who was supposed to be inheriting the Fortress. The sound of clashing metal echoed off the stone walls and other people stopped what they were doing to watch the fencing.

"She will be a very good ruler," continued Agate, watching the pair spar, swords clashing. "Already our father has been sending Mica to trade with the eastern village. She can drive a hard bargain, I've been told."

"So we really are half-sisters," muttered Vancy. It hadn't sunk in that they were related.

"Oh yes."

Her gaze was on Mica and the young man. Even in a dress, Mica was faster than he was. She made feints with her sword that he only just managed to avoid, forcing him slowly back towards the outer wall. Vancy winced. She wouldn't like to fight Mica.

"So why aren't you going to be ruler?" asked Vancy.

"Me!" Agate laughed good-naturedly at the idea. "Why, I shall be married and a mother," she murmured. "It has been decided."

Again, Vancy glanced at the woman's profile, thinking she must be joking. But no, Agate's expression was entirely serious. Vancy shook her head. She didn't understand the Fortress people. Apart from Mica, they were all so submissive, as if they were slaves.

"Oh!" Vancy's hand flew to her mouth. The young man had been nicked by Mica's sword. They stopped sparring and he stood for a moment, white-faced, holding his arm as blood trickled out from between his fingers. Then he bowed and handed the sword, hilt first, back to Mica.

"She always wins," said Agate, getting up and brushing down her skirt.

Unkind thoughts were swarming through Vancy's head, mainly to do with Mica tasting defeat for a change. She followed Agate back towards the great hall. At least now she knew more about Herit's true intentions. But what then was his real plan for *her*?

The three of them sat underneath the tree, watching the sun go down. The sky was a deep purple-blue, laced with golden clouds. The evening star glittered low in the sky and a crescent moon was rising. In silence, they roasted another rabbit over the fire. None of them had the heart to talk about what the silver dog had shown them. To talk about it would make it real, and none of them wanted that.

But talking was inevitable. They couldn't put it off forever.

Tem cleared his throat. "So, it looks like we are here, together, for a reason," he said.

Squirt, who was stretched out on the ground, a piece of grass between his teeth, said nothing. Kerei shuffled, trying to make himself more comfortable, and also said nothing.

Tem continued. "It is obvious that we must do something. The dogs can't fight Herit alone."

"We have done something before, and that didn't work," muttered Squirt, his face unreadable in the dim light.

"True," admitted Tem. "We thought the avalanche was enough to destroy his Fortress, to destroy Herit. I underestimated him. I thought his obsession was only his metal, and that if we destroyed his furnaces it would be enough. But he has obviously found another way to gain power."

Kerei was shaking his head. "I can't believe Vancy has gone to the Fortress," he burst out. "We've got to get her out!"

Tem laid a hand on his shoulder. "Yes, but we also have to think about Bassorah."

"Oh, Bassorah," he snorted. "Bassorah can look after itself. We have to tell Vancy what Herit's planning. Don't you see? She's trapped in there. Anything could happen to her."

"I don't think Herit will hurt her," said Tem. "She is his daughter, after all."

"Kerei's right," came Squirt's steady voice from the grass. The sky was fading to black and the light was turning grey around them. He sat up and threw away his piece of grass. "It's like this. Herit hasn't changed. He's got Vancy there for some reason. We don't know what. But we have to get her out. *Then* we can figure out what to do about Bassorah."

The other two were silent for a moment.

Eventually, Tem spoke. "We must warn them at least," he said quietly.

"Yes," agreed Squirt. "We warn Bassorah, *and* we rescue Vancy."

XI

There was a commotion out in the front courtyard. People who had been eating breakfast crept to the entrance way to peer outside. Vancy had just come down to the great hall after a restless night's sleep, her face washed but barely awake. She spotted Mica and Agate glancing in her direction, but they, too, were heading towards the doors, wanting to see what was happening.

Taking her opportunity, Vancy sidled past one of the many candle holders and slipped out a candle. A quick fumble and it was in her pouch. Then she went to join the others at the door.

Outside, on the flat paved area, she saw Herit first. He wore a long dark robe over trousers, with a silver link belt around his waist. He seemed taller somehow and very stern. A figure cowered at his feet. Vancy watched as Herit raised his fist – and then she saw the long black whip he was holding. As he brought it down on the unfortunate figure huddled below him there was a sigh from the crowd. But the boy – for he could be no more than that, she realised – made no sound. Only flinched.

This was the real Herit, thought Vancy – the cruel tyrant. She was dismayed, all over again, to think that he was her birth father.

Again the whip zipped through the air and came down on the boy's back. Again he flinched. Vancy also flinched. She had never seen anybody whipped. In Bassorah, if you had been disobedient, there were only more chores to do. Or the four-day punishment: cleaning the cobbles while the whole village looked on. Your punishment was one of shame, not physical pain – not like this.

Vancy shuddered and turned away. She couldn't watch any more. She caught Mica's glance, across the heads of the onlookers, and it was one of triumph. Was this something that might be in store for her, too? Mica's look seemed to say so. Or perhaps she just hoped it would be.

Vancy sat at one of the trestle tables and bent her head over a bowl of porridge, but she could only force half of it down. When she took the bowl out to the kitchen, one of the cooks, seeing she was alone, pushed a large leather bucket of food scraps in her direction, and told her to take it out to the kitchen midden. With a sigh, Vancy lifted the heavy bucket and headed out the side door.

The midden, built with small stones, was near the chicken coop. She heaved the smelly contents onto the heap and was about to head back to the kitchen when something caught her eye – a smooth piece of leather. With a stick, Vancy pushed around among the scraps. Her boots!

"Ow," cried Kerei, putting a hand to his head. "I don't remember the tunnel being this low before."

"Just keep moving, will you," muttered Squirt, giving him a shove.

"All right, all right." Kerei set off again, hunched over.

The silver dog was leading them through the tunnels that ran beneath the mountains. They had come this way once before, except they had been travelling away from the Hinterland that time. Now they were going towards it – and towards the Fortress. Vancy had been with them then, too. Already the boys' breathing was laboured. The tunnel, which had been sloping upwards for some time, now levelled out and pinpricks of light from vents in the rock above them provided a dim light.

"Do you think Herit knows about these underground passages?" asked Kerei.

"I hope not," said Squirt. "I wouldn't like to bump into him in a dark tunnel."

"Me neither."

The boys fell silent and for a while the only sound was the scraping of their boots on gravel.

"How do you think Tem will get on?" Kerei asked over his shoulder. Tem had left early that morning, on the mule, bound for Bassorah.

A snort came from behind. "The Council will listen to him . . . " said Squirt, leaving the rest of the sentence unfinished.

"Yeah," Kerei agreed dismally. They would listen to him, then decide that he was quite demented and send him off for bed rest and chamomile tea. After all, ghosts weren't exactly a common occurrence around Bassorah. Children made up stories about them, but Kerei couldn't remember anybody actually seeing one. "There was that time that Blind Hufer said he saw the ghost of a huge white bird hovering over the lake," he said.

Squirt burst out laughing. "Sure. Or the time old Lily saw her husband's ghost."

"But everyone agreed that was a batch of bad cider," said Kerei.

"Course, that's assuming Tem even gets there on that, whatchamacallit, mule," added Squirt.

The dog came to a fork and made a sharp right turn with the boys following quickly. They didn't want to get left behind down here in this rabbit warren. It was dark now and Kerei stumbled on a rock.

"Crivets," he muttered between clenched teeth. How come Squirt never stumbled, while he fell over anything? He was looking forward to getting back outside where he could stand up properly. His neck had a crick in it and the back of his head was lumpy with bruises. The tunnels might be the right size for dogs, but not for lanky humans. And how long had they been in here? It seemed like hours. "I could murder a cheese sandwich," sighed Kerei.

"Maybe you could get Herit to make you one when we get to the Fortress."

"Shut up," he said amiably. "I'll bet you'd like one, too. It's been ages since we ate that bit of cold rabbit for breakfast."

"I've got an apple left," said Squirt.

"Well, all right! Pass it over."

The boys paused while Squirt found the apple, gave it to Kerei, and then they hurried to catch the dog, which was already out of sight. He was waiting for them at another fork in the tunnel illuminated by a shaft of light. The tunnel the dog chose now was even lower than before.

"Oh no," groaned Kerei, sticking the apple between his teeth and dropping to his hands and knees. "Hmpf him herm ug," he added.

"I know exactly what you mean," said Squirt.

Alone at last! Vancy went out through the gates, ignoring the guard in his black leather jerkin and long sword, and wandered off into the Hinterland. There might be only rocks and tussock out here, but at least the air was fresh and she was out in the sunshine. What a change from being stuck inside the dim old Fortress being watched every minute by Mica. It was amazing that she had even got out the way she had, but, after the lunch, Mica had said she could have some free time, perhaps take a walk, she suggested. It seemed too good an opportunity to question, so Vancy had done exactly that.

Walking vaguely towards the east, she wondered about the village Herit had told her about. People at Bassorah would be interested. They might be able to trade with them, too, though it was a fair distance away – probably as far as Tem's village over the mountain range.

Maybe Tem had already arrived home by now. Vancy couldn't help wishing she had gone with him, after all. She hoped one day to visit that village and meet his people – *her* people, too, she remembered. It was where her mother had come from, all those years ago. Funny to think that she'd considered Lisbet and Erik her only family for all that time, only to discover that she already had family living in another village altogether. Yes, one day she would travel over the mountains to that place. Maybe she'd take Kerei and Squirt with her, too. They liked to have adventures . . .

Her reverie was broken by a shout. A guard was jogging across the plain towards her. *Now what?* With a sinking feeling, she noticed that Herit was standing outside the main doors, staring out at the Hinterland – staring at her. She ducked her head and walked back to meet the guard.

Without a word, the guard took her arm and led her quickly back to the Fortress. So she really was a prisoner here, she thought grimly.

Herit, with arms folded, was still waiting for her at the top of the steps. Behind him, in his shadow, was Mica. With a heavy heart, Vancy climbed the steps towards him. She felt suddenly terrified. Would he use his black whip on her, too?

"My daughter," he said in a low voice, "I am displeased with you."

She had reached the level below Herit, and was about to step up and pass him, when his hand flew out, slapping her across the face. Vancy stumbled, nearly falling backwards down the steps, but Herit gripped her arm, just as the guard had done. "It is unsafe for you to walk in the Hinterland," he growled.

Behind him, Mica was smirking.

Vancy put a hand to her burning cheek. "But . . ." she began. *Mica had said it was all right*, she wanted to say, burning with the injustice of it.

Herit held up a hand to silence her. "I will hear no excuses. Go to your room."

There was a patch of light up ahead. The dog had vanished.

"Hey ho," muttered Kerei. "Looks like we're here."

The tunnel had opened out into a larger, flat area like a small room. Above them, a ragged hole gaped in the rock. Kerei grabbed either side of the rock and hauled himself up with Squirt close behind.

Soon, they stood blinking in the harsh light of late afternoon. All around were huge boulders, bigger than the boys.

They were in the foothills above the Hinterland. Below, the grey and brown plains stretched away into infinity. Not a sign of life, except for a distant hawk hovering in the sky, scanning the ground for mice or lizards. In the far distance to their left was the grey-black smudge of the Fortress. Goosebumps sprang up on Kerei's arms. They were foolish idiots, he decided, but it was too late to turn back now. Squirt was also staring at the Fortress. Even his freckles had gone pale: he had to be thinking the same kind of thing as Kerei.

The dog broke the uneasy silence. He nudged each of them in turn, as if to say goodbye. Squirt went to pat him, then pulled back his hand. It didn't seem respectful somehow. The silver dog bowed his head and flicked his ears. Then he jumped back into the hole and was gone.

Kerei sighed. "Well, that's that then."

"Yep," said Squirt, dropping his pack to the ground. "We'd better stay here till it's dark. Then we can make a start."

Vancy waited until she thought the residents of the Fortress would all be asleep before lighting the candle, using a flint she had in her pouch. She laced up her boots (a bit smelly, but still perfectly good). The stone corridor was dark and silent. She turned to her left and followed the corridor down. At the gaping hole in the wall, she lifted her skirt and picked her way carefully around the rubble. The breeze from the hole made the candle flicker, but it didn't go out.

The great hall was empty and dim with only a shaft of moonlight glowing faintly on the floor. Vancy hurried across the room, going around the tables, and entered the far corridor where she had followed Mica and Agate the other day. Counting door openings, she felt her way along the narrow passage. A snore startled her, and she stopped, shielding the candle's light in her hand. Sleeping rooms, she thought. The snoring did not stop, so she continued.

A dark hole opened up on her left. She had reached the steps.

With a hand on one rough wall to steady herself, Vancy crept down the narrow steps. The candle, guttering in the draught, created long shadows on the walls. The steps seemed to go on for a long time and she had forgotten to count them. Just when she thought they would lead her down into the very bowels of the Fortress, she came to a wooden door.

Now what? Should she risk trying to open it? What if somebody was on the other side?

Vancy raised the candle and studied the door and its curved metal handle. Well, what could they do to her anyway? She was already a prisoner in this place. Gingerly, she pushed down on the handle and pulled the door towards her. It opened silently, as if well oiled. Inside was another, wider passage. She must be underneath the great hall by now.

Vancy paused, listening for any sound. It wasn't completely dark down here; a faint light shone up ahead. Vancy shielded the candle with her hand and stepped forward. There was a humming sound, like a swarm of bees. She ought to go back . . . But she was here now and she was curious. She would just see what was at the end of this passage, and then she'd go back to her room.

The passage curved sharply to the right and opened into a large room carved out of the bedrock, like a natural cave. Steps led down into this room, but Vancy held back, staying close to the wall and peering in. The room was lit with large black candles, their flames rising straight to the ceiling. There was no draught down here to make them dance. The humming sound was coming from this room, but there was nothing in it except for a stone table at the far end. Behind the table stood Herit.

Vancy pressed herself further back against the wall, hiding the light of her candle. A feeling of dread ran through her. What was he doing down here in the middle of the night?

As Vancy watched, Herit lifted something and placed it on his head. She squinted. Was it a skull?

Raising both hands, Herit began to chant. She could hear him quite clearly, but did not understand the words. It sounded like gibberish, a foreign language. The strange words shivered through her like ice and a smell of crushed ants filled the room.

Then she noticed the room was not as empty as she had thought: the floor was dotted with skulls. The stone floor was not lit by the candles, so she hadn't noticed them before, but now she could see them because they were glowing.

Herit's chant filled her head and she had a crazy impulse to step forward, to join him – as if his dark words were calling her, pulling her forward. She gripped the rock wall with her free hand, holding herself back.

Transfixed, Vancy could only stare. The room

was wavering and changing, reminding Vancy of the way the fog sometimes swirled over the lake at Bassorah. Shapes were emerging, as if out of the light itself. Dog faces, shifting like water. Legs, and a feeling of running. Sharp barks filled the air.

Suddenly dizzy, Vancy gripped the rock wall, thinking she was outside – in the Hinterland – running with a pack of dogs. She squeezed shut her eyes and took a deep breath. Her head was spinning.

When she next looked, the room was filled with the ghostly shapes of dogs. They sat facing Herit. His chant had stopped now, and the walls themselves seemed to be breathing. Every dog's gaze was fixed on Herit. Silver dogs, but silver dogs who shared one single mind, and, just as the silver dogs communicated by images, so Herit was sending out a picture to this single dog mind.

Vancy's hand flew to her mouth. *Bassorah!*

She turned and fled.

Back up the passageway and through the door. In her hurry, she didn't even think to shut it behind her. She had to get away from this place. She had to warn people. She had to – Vancy gathered up her skirt and flew up the narrow steps. Halfway up, her candle guttered and went out.

Stifling a sob, she pressed a hand against the wall to stop herself from falling backwards. The steps were in complete darkness. With only one thought in her mind, she felt her way up the steps. She had to escape. She would take one of the horses and ride across the Hinterland. If she was lucky, she could be back in Bassorah by dawn.

When she finally reached the top of the steps and staggered out into the corridor she turned right, racing back along the passage. There was the entrance to the great hall. She hurried through it . . . and let out a gasp of fright.

A hand had gripped her wrist. Mica's eyes gleamed in the darkness.

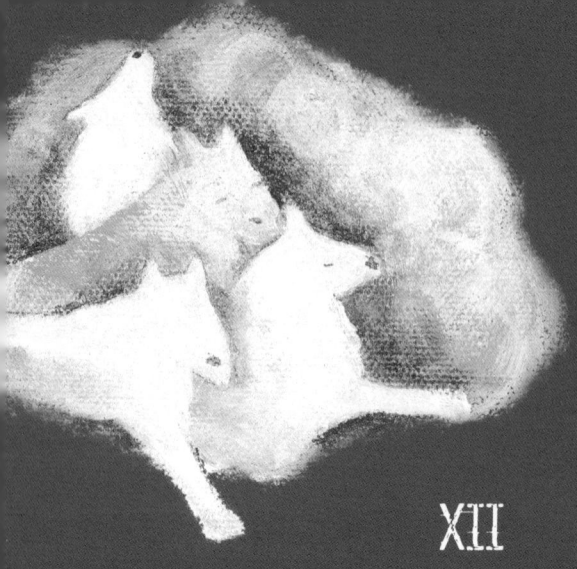

XII

The boys stood in front of a wooden door in the outer wall of the Fortress. They had picked their way down out of the foothills, among stones and thorny bushes, until they reached level ground. A thin moon had offered some light as they headed towards the Fortress and now the sky was lightening towards dawn.

"You ready?" asked Squirt, shouldering his heavy pack.

"Um, no," said Kerei, trying to keep his voice from cracking. His mouth had gone dry at the thought of actually going inside the Fortress.

"Remember that ladder, inside the wall? It'll take us up to the top of the wall. Then we can get down the other side, into that big courtyard area, and run across to the main door."

"Right." Kerei swallowed. He remembered, very

clearly, running with Squirt and Vancy along the passage at the top of the wall, and then finding a trapdoor and a ladder down to this very door.

Squirt was busy examining the door with his fingers. In the dim, grey light, it was hard to see a handle, or any other means of opening it. "We'll have to risk a light," he muttered.

Kerei dug about in his pack and brought out a flint and a tight braid of straw. He struck a flame from the flint and held it to the straw. The light wouldn't last very long, but it should be enough to find the handle. He cupped the flame in his hands and held it close to the door.

The boys studied the smooth, bare surface in silence. There was no handle. No way to open the door from the outside. With a sigh, Kerei snuffed the flame out.

"Well," said Squirt. "That's that then."

"We go back home?" asked Kerei hopefully.

"No, we find another way in."

"I was afraid you'd say that." Kerei shouldered his pack. "I'm going to kill Vancy when I find her," he added. "So what do we do now?"

Squirt was craning his head back to study the looming stone wall. It was three times as tall as a man, with no handholds – impossible to scale.

"There's no other way in except for the main gates," he muttered.

"Where there is an armed sentry," said Kerei drily.

Making no reply, Squirt had started creeping in that direction.

"I hate it when you do that," muttered Kerei, following.

The boys crept up to the edge of the gate, until they could see the black-clad sentry pacing back and forth in the middle of the entrance way.

"Tell you what," whispered Squirt. "I'll distract him while you run inside."

"How're you going to do that? Go over and ask if he's got a sister?"

"I don't know," hissed Squirt. "I haven't thought of anything yet."

"Why don't we throw some stones over there." Kerei pointed at a thorny bush to the far side of the gates. "The guard'll think there's something in that bush, go over and have a look. Then we can run inside."

Squirt frowned at the bush. Even if the guard did go and investigate the bush, it was too close to the gates. They wouldn't have time to slip past him. The boys were still pondering when they heard hurried footsteps within and a voice speaking a name. The guard responded, moving away from the gate and back into the courtyard.

" . . . he wants you to be ready to leave within the hour," said a woman's voice.

"But m'lady, my post . . . "

"Somebody else is coming to take your place," said the brisk voice. "He wants you, so you must go."

"Yes, m'lady."

Footsteps moving away, the voices growing fainter. Something about horses.

"Here's our chance," said Squirt. He grabbed Kerei's arm and dragged the boy after him through the gates.

"Oh, crivets," gasped Kerei.

They pressed themselves into the shadow against the inside of the wall. The paved area spread out before them, murky grey. They were directly opposite the main entrance doors to the Fortress, through which the woman was just disappearing. The guard was heading off around to the right. Nobody else was in sight.

"Let's see if there's a way in over there," Squirt whispered. He ran – across the large paved area, veering around to the left side of the building. Kerei had no choice but to follow.

"I have found a little mouse," said Mica, bundling Vancy into the underground room.

"Ah, my daughter," said Herit smoothly and without surprise. "My *other* daughter," he added. The light shining through the skull on his head made outrageous shadows over his face. The ghostly dogs still sat facing him, shimmering silver and black. Vancy held back, not wanting to be pushed through those ghostly shapes, but Mica pulled her by the wrist along one side of the room and up to the table.

"You have done well, Mica," said Herit. "It is sooner than I had planned, but now that she is here we may as well proceed."

"Let me go," hissed Vancy, struggling in the other woman's grip.

Herit laughed softly. "Yes, Mica, release your stepsister."

With a grimace, Mica let go of Vancy and walked back to the doorway, where she positioned herself to stand guard. Vancy, rubbing at her sore wrist, could see there would be no easy escape.

"What we have here," continued Herit, as if he were explaining the architecture of the Fortress, "is a meeting of minds." He gestured at the ghostly dogs. "My friends, as you can see, are awaiting my orders. I am now, so to speak, the leader of the pack. And you have arrived just in time to show them everything they need to know about Bassorah."

Vancy had backed up against the rock wall, as far away from Herit as she could. Mentally, she ran through the things in her pouch, to see if there was a weapon she could use. Her knife! But could she get it out in time? And would it be of much use against a grown man, when it was made to peel fruit?

"I had planned to collect some more dogs before I made use of your talents. Only a few more days, and we would have had a fine army. But perhaps we have enough for my purpose."

His eyes glittered darkly; above them, the light shining on the skull – Vancy realised with horror that it was that of a dog – seemed to give him two sets of eyes. Following her gaze, Herit touched a hand to the skull. "Isn't it magnificent? It is the oldest dog in the pack. Once an ancient and venerable beast, and now, a fearsome adversary. You shall see."

"You can't make me do anything I don't want to," cried Vancy.

"Really? How interesting you should think that."

Herit reached forward and gripped her wrist, dragging her over to the table. Her hand flew out to stop herself slamming into the stone, and met with a slippery surface. Vancy pulled back in horror: it was blood. A metallic stench filled her nostrils.

She struggled to break free of his grip. But, in a flash, Herit had gripped her head between both his hands, as if in a vice. He turned her towards the dogs. "You will show them," Herit hissed into her ear. "Show them where they will be going."

Vancy struggled, trying not to look, but the deep eyes of the silver dogs stared directly into her mind. She shut her eyes, but still she saw them. With Herit's fingers pressing into her temples, Vancy grew limp, mesmerised.

Running . . . running like a dog across the barren wastes of the Hinterland. A leader out in front, as fast as the wind. Vancy, in the middle of the pack, flying across the ground. Time and space fell away behind her. Stars glittered in a black sky, then snuffed out like candles. Up ahead were the ragged cliffs of Bassorah. A Patrol appeared, then fell back in terror, men rolling helplessly on the ground. The entrance to the Pass appeared and the pack rushed through it like a fierce wind. There was the Keep, looming up. More men appeared, but fell back like the others. Here was the cobbled street that ran up between the houses . . .

Vancy gasped, struggling to fight back. But it was no good. She couldn't stop Bassorah from appearing in her mind, as solid as wood, clear in every detail. The street, the houses, the people who lived in the houses, stepping out to see what was happening: here was the entire community, exposed.

Bells rang, children screamed. People reeled back in horror.

The dog pack rushed through, continuous and unstoppable . . . until the entire community was destroyed by fear. This, Vancy realised, was the message that Herit wanted the dogs to see.

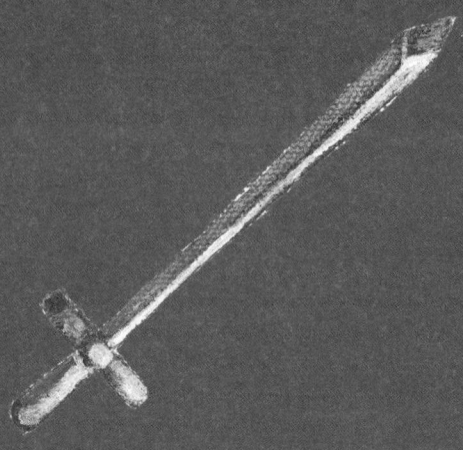

XIII

The boys crouched in the shadow of the Fortress itself.

They could see the new sentry now, pacing back and forth across the gate entrance. A bird called in the night, making Kerei jump, but there was no other sound. Squirt crept along the wall with Kerei following. It wasn't long before they discovered a small outer door, unlocked. Squirt cautiously pulled it open then paused, listening.

No movement from within. The boys went up some steps and found themselves in a stone passage. "Which way?" whispered Kerei.

Squirt looked in both directions, listening intently. No wonder he'd been taken on at the Keep, thought Kerei. This kind of creeping around seemed to come naturally to him. Squirt nodded to his right and the boys crept stealthily along the corridor. They passed doorways, pausing at each to listen. The whole place seemed to be asleep.

At the end of the corridor was an arched doorway, beyond which the boys could make out a huge, high-ceilinged room. A shaft of moonlight fell across a single long trestle table. They had never seen such a large room.

Suddenly, they heard the sound of footsteps. "Someone's coming," hissed Squirt, pressing himself back against the rock wall.

"I have already said no," came a deep voice. A man appeared at the other end of the great hall, carrying a large bundle in his arms. He was followed by a young woman who seemed to be appealing to him – imploring, nagging. Her words drifted across the room to the boys.

"But father," she was saying, "I can help you."

"You are a fine swordswoman," replied the man. Kerei gasped – it was Herit! "But I need you to stay here. Somebody must keep order while I am gone."

Now the woman said something the boys couldn't hear.

"Listen to me, Mica," snapped Herit, turning on her. "If we are both gone, anything might happen here. The people need firm and constant leadership. You are my daughter and I am telling you that you will stay." He lowered his bundle onto the long table.

Squirt glanced back at Kerei. "It's a body," he whispered. Kerei nodded, wide-eyed.

Herit was speaking more gently to the woman now. "It won't take very long and I will send for you as soon as it is over. Then you shall join me – in Bassorah. Watch for a silver dog."

"Yes, father," murmured the woman.

"What's on his head?" whispered Kerei.

"Dunno," responded Squirt.

The boys watched breathlessly as Herit strode towards the huge doors and, one at a time, swung them open. Outside came the rattle of horses' hooves on stone. Herit gave a single high-pitched whistle. The shrill sound echoed around the room and seemed to spiral deep into the Fortress. It was followed by a rushing sound, like a wind rattling through corn stalks.

"What the . . . " muttered Kerei, goggling.

A silver-grey cloud appeared in the hall, moving towards Herit. It looked as if it might swallow him up, but the man merely held up his hand, and the cloud stopped at his command. He stepped back, and it rushed past him and out through the doors, swirling into the night. Herit swiftly followed.

Kerei felt Squirt grab his arm. "What's she doing?" his friend whispered.

At the table, the woman standing by the prone body was drawing something from the folds of her dress – something that flashed in the shaft of moonlight.

"It's a sword," hissed Squirt.

With a determined look, the woman raised the sword above her head.

Without thinking, Squirt took off, running across the room and hurtling over the table. There was a moment when the woman realised she was not alone and began to turn. Then, still sliding, Squirt grabbed the sword from her and pushed her aside. She crumpled to the ground with the force of their collision.

When Kerei caught up with Squirt, he was standing over her, sword in hand.

"That's a woman, you know," muttered Kerei.

Squirt looked down, horrified, at the woman lying unconscious at their feet. "Do you think I've killed her?"

"Don't be silly. You can't kill somebody by colliding with them."

"But she might've hit her head on the ground," whispered Squirt.

A groan from the bundle on the table diverted

their attention. Squirt walked over and drew away the rough cloth that covered the body. "Vancy!" he murmured, amazed.

"Can't be," said Kerei, peering over his shoulder, "she's wearing a dress." They leaned closer. "No, it's definitely Vancy." He started shaking her shoulders. "Hey, Vancy, wake up!"

"Don't do that," hissed Squirt. He dropped the sword and bent over her. "She might be hurt."

"Here," said Kerei, "I've got some water left," and, before Squirt could stop him, he had dashed cold water into Vancy's face.

She gasped and moaned, rolling onto her side.

"You idiot," hissed Squirt. "What did you do that for?"

"That's how you get somebody to wake up," protested Kerei. "My mother does it to me all the time."

"This isn't you snoring away in your bed!" said Squirt.

"No, but it works. See . . . "

Vancy had opened her eyes and was staring up at them. Was she dreaming? She thought it was Kerei and Squirt standing there bickering, but that couldn't be – they were back in Bassorah. *Bassorah!* She sat up suddenly, then clutched her head and groaned.

"Vancy?" murmured Squirt. "Are you all right?"

She swung her legs off the table. "Of course I'm not all right," she snapped. "Come on, we have to hurry!" Gathering up her skirt, she ran towards the entrance way.

The boys hurried after her. "Vancy, wait," hissed Kerei behind her. "Where are we going?"

No response. They were running around to the left of the Fortress towards a stone fence with a wooden gate, through which Vancy was flying. The boys stumbled after her. Up ahead, something whinnied and there was a flurry of movement. Kerei goggled as they rushed past a small pony-like beast with very long ears. Now Vancy had grabbed something from a hook and was throwing it over the head of an extremely large pony.

"Crivets," muttered Kerei. "What under the gods is that?"

Squirt was grinning; the rising sun flashed on his white teeth and turned his unruly thatch of hair to gold. "I do believe that is one half of our beast."

"What, a greathorse?"

"Yep."

But there was no time to admire the creature, which had begun to stamp its huge front hooves and roll its eyes.

"Stupid dress," muttered Vancy, hitching it up. Then she grabbed the horse by its mane and swung herself up onto the back of the restless animal. Knotting the reins around her hand, she had begun to turn its head towards the open gate when she remembered the boys, who stood staring up at her, open-mouthed. She reached a hand down to Squirt. "Up you get ... use my foot." She had curled up her foot to make a step for him.

With a wide grin, Squirt swung up easily behind Vancy then reached down for Kerei. The beast was so big, there was enough room for the three of them.

"Oh no," said Kerei, shaking his head. "There's no way you're going to get me on ... "

A shout came from the dark Fortress.

"Hurry up, Kerei," hissed Vancy. "They're coming!"

The boy grabbed Squirt's outstretched hand and struggled awkwardly up onto the horse. "This is the thanks we get," he was muttering. "Bossed around, made to get up on this giant pony ... "

"Hang on!" cried Vancy, kicking her heels into the flanks of the horse.

The boys didn't need to be told twice, as the horse, with a snort, took off at a jog, heading for the gate in the stone fence.

XIV

"Oh my heart," Kerei was muttering, clinging on to Squirt as if his life depended on it. "I'll never get over this."

They were jogging across the Hinterland, the Fortress falling rapidly behind them. A staccato conversation had been taking place between Squirt and Vancy as they travelled. "And then we heard about the ghost army . . ."

"I *saw* it," gasped Vancy, still shocked by what she had seen. "It was awful."

"And Tem went back to warn Bassorah . . ."

"Don't know how much good that will do," said Vancy. "They won't believe him."

Her hair was flicking in his face, but Squirt didn't seem to mind. "That's what I thought, too."

Nubby jogged on tirelessly, across the tussocky plains.

"Listen, Vancy," said Squirt, feeling as if he had to tell her this. "That woman with Herit, she was going to kill you . . . "

Vancy was silent for a moment, as if she hadn't heard. Finally, she said: "That is Herit's daughter."

"I'm guessing she doesn't like you too much," suggested Squirt.

Mica truly *was* Herit's daughter, thought Vancy, in a way that she could never be, or want to be.

"What are you talking about?" called Kerei, left out of the conversation.

"Van says you're a great oaf and we'd go faster if we tipped you off."

"She did not!"

Squirt was grinning again.

"Uh-oh," muttered Kerei. "With all this bouncing up and down, I need to . . . you know."

Squirt told Vancy, but she only spurred the horse on into a canter. "He'll have to wait," she said grimly.

When they did stop – Vancy hauling on the reins and calling out to the horse – it was not for Kerei (who hurried off behind a bush) but for Nubby. The horse was frothing at the mouth.

"Do you have any water?" she asked Squirt.

He dug in his pack and brought out his water skin. Vancy made a bowl for the horse to drink from by linking her hands beneath the fabric of her skirt. "There, there," she murmured, "good boy." It wasn't perfect, but with luck it would be enough to keep the horse going.

"How did you learn to ride one of these great-horses?" asked Squirt, with obvious admiration.

Diverted from her thoughts of Herit's ghost army and the fate of Bassorah, Vancy blushed. "I didn't learn. Not exactly, but I've ridden the mill ponies, just around the edges of the fields, to try and tame them. I figured it'd be the same kind of thing with a horse." She scuffed her foot against a rock and a small lizard went skittering away. Nubby was grazing on grasses between the rocks. "Actually, it's completely different. Just don't tell Kerei I said so," she finished with a wry grin.

"Your secret's safe with me," said Squirt, now blushing himself.

"Hey ho," said Kerei, coming back. "Has anybody got anything to eat?" They both looked at him and burst out laughing. "What?" he cried, indignant.

"You," said Vancy, smiling for the first time in days. There might be a ghost army about to attack Bassorah, but Kerei could always be relied on to think of his stomach.

"What *about* me?" he asked. "It was a perfectly

reasonable question." But Vancy made no reply. She was already swinging back up onto the horse. "Horses," groaned Kerei. "Dangerous at both ends and uncomfortable in the middle!"

It was late in the day when Vancy noticed a dark line in the distance, running out from the mountains. The cliffs of Bassorah, she thought grimly. Would they be too late? She hung onto the horse tighter with her knees, spurring the horse on faster. Against the sky, now silver from the setting sun, she could make out another pale shape, like a piece of cut-out fog on the grey-brown plains of the Hinterland. At its centre was the dark figure of a rider.

"Squirt," she called back over her shoulder. "Was Herit alone?"

"We didn't see him go outside," he replied, "but I think there was another man with him." He, too, was squinting into the distance. "Is that it – the ghost army?"

Vancy nodded. They were drawing closer and closer and her heart was pounding in her chest. She had no idea how they were going to stop Herit. She had been so focused on catching up, she hadn't taken the time to think about what would happen once they did. But, now they were approaching Bassorah, Vancy realised how helpless they really were. How did you stop a pack of demented ghost dogs? Yet she knew the dogs were good creatures . . . no matter how completely Herit might be controlling them. Underneath they were still the mighty silver dogs of the plains. Now another thought wormed its way into her mind. These weren't real dogs. These were the ghosts of dogs. Trembling with fright and horror, Vancy would have given anything to turn back.

"What's that?" called Kerei from behind. "In front of the Pass?"

Vancy squinted beyond the wavery, fog-like shape of the ghost pack. There were figures in front of the Pass and it looked as if the pack had stopped. Would Bassorah have had enough warning to bring out one of the Patrols? A chill ran through Vancy. Kerei's mother, she remembered, was in the Patrols. Vancy prayed that Merta wasn't outside now, facing a nightmare attack.

"What're we going to do?" cried Squirt.

She could hear the fear in his voice. But there was something else as well. She glanced back at the staunch face at her shoulder. Bravery, she realised, and, with that realisation, something clicked into place in Vancy's mind. She wasn't alone.

She reined in the horse, speaking softly to it until it had slowed to a stop.

"What's happening?" came a complaining voice.

"There's too much weight," said Vancy, looking back at them. "I'm going on by myself."

"No," said Squirt. "We're staying together."

Kerei was already sliding off the horse.

Vancy eyed Squirt steadily. "I . . . I've got a plan," she muttered. "I want you two to go around the side of the pack. Around there." She turned and pointed to the right of the milling dogs, Herit in their midst. "I want you to create a diversion."

"And where are you going to be?" asked Squirt, frowning at her back.

"Don't worry about me," said Vancy.

"I'm not going," he said.

But now he was being tugged off the horse by Kerei, who had taken a firm grip on his ankle. "Hey! Leggo!" shouted Squirt as he tumbled to the ground.

"You heard Vancy," Kerei was saying. "She's got a plan."

Squirt had struggled out of Kerei's grip, but it was too late. Vancy had kicked the horse forward.

"You, you . . . " spluttered Squirt.

"Shut up," said Kerei, shrugging his pack off his

back. "Now come on, we have to hurry." And he took off at a run, veering away to the north. It was Squirt's turn to follow.

As she drew closer to Bassorah, it was clear what was happening: the Patrol was guarding the Pass and trying to hold off Herit – for now. One of Herit's guard was on the ground, speaking with the Patrol, his horse tethered several paces away against the cliffs. The man was gesturing to the ghostly pack behind him. Tem was there, too – pale, but stern. He lifted his head at the sound of her horse's hooves. Merta, too, looked up. Seeing who was coming, she shook her head. She was shouting something that sounded like, "*Get back!*"

But Vancy had no intention of getting back. She came on, relaxing her hold on the reins, around to the left of the ghostly pack.

Herit, sitting on a horse in the midst of the eerie dogs, also turned to see who was coming. His eyes were black beneath the dog skull on his head. He flashed her a look of such hatred, Vancy gasped in fear. As if picking up on her sudden loss of nerve, Nubby checked himself, then reared. Caught off guard, Vancy tumbled to the ground and swiftly rolled away from his stamping hooves. The horse, eyes rolling, turned and galloped back the way they had come.

Vancy got up and dusted herself off. Luckily she hadn't landed on any rocks. Something caught her eye – a movement. It was Kerei and Squirt, running in a large arc around the far side of the pack. She turned to face Herit.

"Ah, my daughter," cried Herit, hiding his hatred behind his triumph. "You've come to join me, I see. We shall enter Bassorah together!" His horse was prancing and rolling its eyes with fear as the ghost dogs milled around behind him, shimmering silver, as if waiting for a signal. "We are just talking to these good people of yours," he continued, "offering them the chance to surrender."

Vancy bit her lip as she inched forward. *They are only ghosts*, she told herself sternly. *Only air and vapours. They can't hurt me. They can't hurt me.* Icy air flowed around Vancy as she moved through the ghostly dogs, forcing herself to face the glimmering teeth that seemed to snarl, then recede. Cold dog bodies pressed against her. She had the fleeting sense that the dogs were reading her, trying to see if she was friend or foe.

"I'm your *friend*," she muttered between gritted teeth.

But, like telling a wild dog to be calm, it seemed to make no difference. If these were real dogs, possessed by Herit's evil will, they would rip her apart.

"Yes, my brave daughter," Herit was saying, watching her progress. "We shall rule Bassorah together. Would you like that? Unless, of course, you have come to save your precious Bassorah? In which case," he murmured, with a thin smile, "I would have no choice but to set these dogs upon you."

She found herself shaking, whether from the cold or fear, it was hard to say. Yet her eyes never left his face.

"Do you think I could do that, daughter?"

Vancy nodded. "You are most powerful," she murmured, not knowing where the words had come from.

His black eyes drew her on – mesmerising, deep as wells. She was getting close now to those stamping hooves. Herit's horse, trembling with fear, was only just under control.

"Ah, my daughter. Without you, I am nothing," murmured Herit, his smile broader now, confident in his power. But that cruel smile told a lie.

Nevertheless, she grasped his outstretched hand and swung up quickly, bravely, behind him. His hot whisper burned her face as he turned back towards her. "Together, we shall be invincible. I shall be King and you will rule with me!"

Pride flooded through Vancy. It was true: she would be with her real father. They would rule together. Nobody would look down on her again. She would punish the proud Bassorah people who had sent her away. She would be powerful, just like her father.

Herit turned to face the Patrol. His guard had stepped away, shaking his head. Now the Patrol had raised their spears. How puny they looked. From her vantage point on Herit's horse, Vancy could see their hesitation. Once again, Herit was using the situation to his advantage. They would be worried about hurting her if they charged. Tem, too, was frowning, anxious. Merta looked furious. She could see Herit tensing to push the horse forward.

Just then, there came a wild whoop. All heads turned.

Two boys, arms pumping, came running up from the right, shouting their heads off.

Vancy shook herself. *Where was she?*

She felt the nervous horse moving beneath her. There was a moment's confusion, and then she remembered. *Crivets*, she'd been about to attack Bassorah with Herit! The man himself loomed large in front of her, the horrid dog skull making a monster of him. A not-man, and there she had been, thinking about being ruler of Bassorah! A rush of bitter bile filled her mouth. The boys were shouting and madly waving their arms. Everything was confusion, but a confusion that wouldn't last for long.

Swallowing down the bile, Vancy raised her arms and took a firm grip on the dog's skull on Herit's head. For a split second, he began to turn his head at the touch. Then she had ripped it away and thrown it hard into the air. It rose and fell in a smooth arc, and then landed on a rock, smashing into a hundred tiny pieces.

"*You!*" Herit roared. He was turned towards her, his eyes blazing with fury, but something else was happening now – something she couldn't see. The world had begun to spin upside-down, and she, too, was flying through the air. As she landed with a thump that knocked the wind out of her, Vancy caught a glimpse of Herit's horse rearing above the snapping ghost dogs. Then she blacked out.

XV

Voices, murmuring. A sense of light. A bird twittering in the distance. *I am in a garden,* thought Vancy, as if seeing herself from above. The sound of falling water. *A garden with a waterfall.* She had always wanted to sleep next to a waterfall. And so warm. Must be summer. Bees buzzing, crickets singing, and voices conversing, low and soft, words drifting at the very edge of her consciousness, making no sense, just pure sound.

Gradually, random words started to appear in her mind like bubbles. *Cheating . . . not so . . . up your sleeve . . . roll again . . . don't be so . . .*

Vancy blinked. Light stung her eyes and she shut them again. It was a dream, she told herself. When she looked again, the details began to come into focus. She saw a ceiling, a familiar ceiling. But how was it familiar? A wave of dizziness made her shut her eyes again. The voices continued faintly.

"So you're ockle and I'm bockie . . ."

"But I was ockle before."

"No, you were nunckle . . ."

"Not so, nunckle."

"Yes so!"

She opened her eyes again and smiled weakly.

Kerei and Squirt were on the floor, moving in and out of focus, playing peaknuckle. Glancing up, Kerei saw that she was awake and nudged Squirt. Soon they were both peering at her, as if she were some kind of exotic beetle. Vancy had an idea she might be grinning. She tried to say, *Where am I?* But, even though her lips were moving, no sound came out.

"She's trying to say something," whispered Kerei.

"Go get Lisbet," said Squirt.

Kerei disappeared. She felt Squirt, looking anxious, take her hand. She tried to smile again, but her mouth wasn't working any more. *What was Squirt's real name*, she wondered vaguely.

Mist drifted across her eyes, and she sank once more into unconsciousness.

"And then," Kerei was saying eagerly, "the mighty warriors came racing into the scene . . . and Herit was so terrified that he fell off his horse."

"You're spitting," said Squirt, wiping his face with his sleeve. "You know I hate that."

"Wait," murmured Vancy. "Slow down. You're making my head hurt."

Vancy sat propped up in bed nursing a mug of cool water, wrapped in Lisbet's soft winter shawl. The two boys were sitting on either side of the bed.

Squirt took up the story. "What *really* happened," he said, "is that you ripped off that skull he was wearing and everything went crazy. The dogs sort of woke up and didn't know what to do. The horse was bucking and standing on its back legs, and you went flying off the horse . . . "

"Flying through the air," crowed Kerei. "You should've seen it!"

"How could she have seen it, radish brain? She was the one it was happening to," said Squirt. "And stop spitting. I hate that."

"You landed so hard, everybody thought you'd been knocked dead."

"If I could continue . . . "

"Nobody's stopping you," huffed Kerei.

"Then Herit fell off the horse. And it was as if…" Squirt hesitated, frowning. He glanced at Kerei, who had developed a sudden interest in something outside the window. "Kerei? You tell her."

The boy cleared his throat, looking suddenly haunted. "It was as if," Kerei said softly, "it was as if Herit was being ripped apart by a pack of dogs."

They were all silent. Vancy, her eyes wide with shock, didn't know whether she felt horrified or relieved. Finally, she asked the one thing she had to know: "Is he dead?"

Kerei nodded. Squirt was looking at his hands. "It was just as well you didn't see it," he muttered. "It was horrible." He looked up. "The strange thing is, they weren't real – I know that – but, for a moment, they *did* become real . . ."

The boys exchanged a glance, and Kerei shook his head, as if they had said too much. "Anyway," he continued. "They just vanished, poof, like that. All that was left was Herit's body."

"Except," said Squirt quickly, "when Merta went over to look, there wasn't a mark on him. He was just stone dead."

Silence filled the room. Finally, Vancy took a deep breath and then sighed it out. "You know something? I'm glad he's dead." There wasn't anything they could say to that.

"Anyway," said Kerei, "you're officially a hero now. The Council are practically falling over themselves to make you an assistant."

"To the Council?" Since she had woken up, it seemed that she had been hearing one unbelievable thing after another. "Me?"

"Yep," said Kerei. "It's been years since they last made anybody an assistant."

"But I'm only fifteen."

Just then, Erik appeared in the doorway. "Time for the patient to rest now, boys."

They stood up reluctantly and Squirt hung back, promising to drop by in the evening to see how she was getting along. "I'll bring some berries," he said.

Vancy reached up and held his hand for a moment. "Thanks," she said, and was just about to call him Squirt when she remembered the thought she had had in her dazed state. "What's your real name?"

"Yager," he said in a low voice.

"Come now," said Erik, good-naturedly. "All this excitement won't be helping the patient."

"Thank you, Yager," said Vancy.

He blushed to the roots of his ginger hair.

Vancy was inside the ponies' enclosure, doling out greens from a bucket. She was still prone to sudden headaches and dizzy spells, but each day she could feel herself getting a little stronger. As if sensing a new fragility in the girl, the ponies were not their usual boisterous selves. They nudged her gently and seemed careful to create some space around her, rather than crowding her as they usually did. She scratched one behind the ears, stroked another's velvety snout. They nibbled at the leaves as she presented them, nipping at each other when any of them became too pushy.

She smiled. It was good to be back among animals that were shorter than she was. Although the guard's horse had been kept at Bassorah, stabled with the mule, Vancy didn't think she'd want to ride it. Well, not for a while, at any rate. Nobody knew what had happened to Herit's horse. She hoped it had found its way home with Nubby. It was Squirt who was looking after the greathorse and teaching himself how to ride.

"They look happy to see you again," said a voice behind her.

Vancy turned to find Tem leaning against the stone wall.

"You think so?" she asked, letting herself out of

the gate and hanging the empty bucket back on its hook.

"I know so. How are you feeling?"

She shrugged. "All right." She squinted at him in the sunlight. "Will you be going soon?"

"Yes," he said. "Now that I know you are better, I'll probably leave for my village quite soon. I've been away from home far too long."

"Maybe you won't recognise anybody," she teased.

"Maybe so," said Tem. "They'll be wondering about this stranger named Tem who's arrived in their village."

They started walking slowly down the cobbled road between the houses, heading towards Vancy's house. "Will you come back again?" she asked, feeling sad that she might not see her uncle again for a long time.

He put a hand on her shoulder. "Just try and keep me away," he said, trying to make light of it. "Ah, but here is your faithful companion."

Vancy looked up to see Squirt – Yager – waiting outside her house. Her face went hot and she glanced down at the cobbles. Then she looked up again and smiled. Yager smiled back. He looked taller, somehow, and older, and that was how she felt herself. It seemed years ago now that she had had her coming-of-age party. Years ago that she'd been a silly girl of fifteen. Vancy wondered what the future held for her – for all of them – now that Herit was dead. She hoped it meant the beginning of a long period of peace.

Tem was wading through fine grass up to his hips, as if wading through water. Ahead of him, the grass swished and parted as a large silver dog moved through it, stately and dignified, leading the way. Tem raised his face to the sun, smiling. It felt good to be back in this land beyond the Hinterland: a fortunate land.

Eventually, the grass became shorter, until man and dog were walking side by side between sparse but shady trees. They came to a place where the land sloped away into the distance – a vista of green valleys and ridges, trees and a distant line of forest. Somewhere over there lay Tem's village, and the thought filled him with an eager anticipation – *home*.

Tem put his hand on the dog's shoulder. "Well, old friend," he murmured, "I'll say goodbye here." It was the border of the dogs' territory.

The silver dog bowed his head, and gave a single bark. With a last glance at Tem, he loped away, back towards the golden, grassy plains.